Growing Lavender

The Ultimate Guide to Planting, Growing and Caring for Lavenders along with Making the Most of This Herb in Cooking, Aromatherapy, and Crafting

© Copyright 2021

The contents of this book may not be reproduced, duplicated, or transmitted without direct written permission from the author.

Under no circumstances will any legal responsibility or blame be held against the publisher for any reparation, damages, or monetary loss due to the information herein, either directly or indirectly.

Legal Notice:

You cannot amend, distribute, sell, use, quote, or paraphrase any part of the content within this book without the author's consent.

Disclaimer Notice:

Please note the information contained within this document is for educational and entertainment purposes only. No warranties of any kind are expressed or implied. Readers acknowledge that the author is not engaging in the rendering of legal, financial, medical, or professional advice. Please consult a licensed professional before attempting any techniques outlined in this book.

By reading this document, the reader agrees that under no circumstances is the author responsible for any losses, direct or indirect, which are incurred as a result of the use of the information contained within this document, including, but not limited to, errors, omissions, or inaccuracies.

Contents

INTRODUCTION 1
CHAPTER 1: AN INTRODUCTION TO LAVENDER 3
   PRACTICAL, THERAPEUTIC, AND MEDICINAL USES OF LAVENDER 6
      Acne 6
      Dry Skin and Eczema 7
      Skin Lightening 7
      Face Wrinkles 8
      Anti-Inflammatory Use 8
      Wound-Healing Use 8
      Insect Repellent 8
   CULINARY USES 10
CHAPTER 2: DIFFERENT TYPES OF LAVENDER 12
   FRENCH LAVENDER (LAVANDULA DENTATA) 13
   BALLERINA (LAVANDULA STOECHAS) 14
   KEW RED (LAVENDER STOECHAS) 15
   ANOUK (LAVENDER STOECHAS) 16
   BETTY'S BLUE (LAVANDULA ANGUSTIFOLIA) 17
   LAVENITE PETITE (LAVANDULA ANGUSTIFOLIA) 18
   HIDCOTE (LAVANDULA ANGUSTIFOLIA) 19

IMPRESS PURPLE (LAVANDULA X INTERMEDIA) 20
HIDCOTE GIANT (LAVANDULA X INTERMEDIA) 21
GROSSO (LAVANDULA X INTERMEDIA) 22
PORTUGUESE LAVENDER (LAVANDULA LATIFOLA) 23
EGYPTIAN LAVENDER (LAVANDULA MULTIFIDA) 24
THE BEST LAVENDER FOR YOU 24
 English Lavender 24
 Lavandin Hybrids 25
 French Lavender 25
 Spanish Lavender 25
WHAT LAVENDER CAN DO FOR YOU 26
 Best Lavender for Perennial Gardens 26
 Best Lavender for Humid, Hot Climates 26
 Best Cold-Hardy Lavender 27
 Best Compact Lavender Plants 27
 Best Fragrant Lavender for Drying and Preserving 28
 Best Lavender for Containers 29
 Best Lavenders for Pollinator Gardens 29
 Best Lavender For Topiaries 30
 The Best Lavender for Hedges and Knot Gardens 31
 Best Culinary Lavender 31

CHAPTER 3: HOW TO PLANT LAVENDER AND CARE FOR IT 32
CHOOSING PLANTS BY ZONE 32
 Southern Climates 33
 Northern Climates 34
GROWING YOUR LAVENDER OUTDOORS 34
CHOOSING AND PREPARING YOUR PLANTING SITE 37
CARING FOR YOUR LAVENDER 38
GROWING LAVENDER IN CONTAINERS 40
CARING FOR LAVENDER IN CONTAINERS 43

CHAPTER 4: LAVENDER DISEASES AND PESTS 44

SPITTLEBUGS 44
   How to Control Spittlebugs *45*
WHITEFLIES 46
   How to Control Whiteflies *46*
APHIDS 47
   How to Prevent Alfalfa Mosaic Virus *47*
ROOT ROT 48
LAVENDER SHAB 49
COMPANION PLANTING 50
FIVE COMPANION PLANTS FOR LAVENDER 52
HOW TO REVIVE A DYING LAVENDER PLANT 53
   Identify the Problem *54*
   Root Rot *55*
   Leggy Lavender with Yellow Foliage *56*
   Woody Growth *58*
HOW TO REVIVE WOODY LAVENDER 59
HOW TO REVIVE LAVENDER IN A CONTAINER 60
HOW TO REVIVE SHADED LAVENDER 61
HOW TO REVIVE LAVENDER AFTER WINTER 62

CHAPTER 5: HOW TO PRUNE LAVENDER PLANTS 64
   WHY YOU SHOULD PRUNE LAVENDER 64
   Pruning English Lavender *65*
   Pruning Hybrid Lavender *65*
   Pruning Spanish Lavender *66*
   WHEN TO PRUNE LAVENDERS 67
   PRUNING TOOLS 68
   PRUNING TECHNIQUES 69
   PRUNING LAVENDER IN SPRING 69
   PRUNING LAVENDER IN SUMMER 70
   TIPS FOR PRUNING LAVENDER 72

CHAPTER 6: HARVESTING AND STORING LAVENDER 73

WHEN TO HARVEST LAVENDER 74
WHICH FLOWERS TO HARVEST 75
HOW TO DRY YOUR LAVENDER FLOWERS 77
    Hanging Lavender 77
    Using a Food Dehydrator 79
    In Baskets or on Screens 80
    In the Oven 81
    In the Microwave 82
STORING DRIED LAVENDER 82

CHAPTER 7: SIMPLE LAVENDER GIFTS AND CRAFTS 84
LAVENDER SACHETS – NO-SEW 84
LAVENDER BALL 87
LAVENDER WANDS 89
LAVENDER HEARTS 94
REUSABLE LAVENDER DRYER BAGS 101
LAVENDER WREATH 102
LAVENDER AND LIME POTPOURRI 105
WEDDING CONFETTI CONES 107
LAVENDER CHRISTMAS BALL ORNAMENTS 109
LAVENDER EYE PILLOW 110
LAVENDER FIRE BUNDLES 112

CHAPTER 8: COOKING WITH LAVENDER 114
WHAT MAKES LAVENDER "CULINARY?" 114
HOW TO USE LAVENDER IN COOKING 117
LAVENDER SHORTBREAD 120

LAVENDER SUGAR 123
LAVENDER-INFUSED HONEY 125
LAVENDER HONEY ICE CREAM 126
ROAST CHICKEN GLAZED WITH LAVENDER HONEY 128
LAVENDER SORBET 129
BERRY SALAD WITH A LEMON LAVENDER VINAIGRETTE 131

LAVENDER AND PEPITA BRITTLE... 133
LAVENDER LEMONADE 135
LAVENDER SPRITZER... 137
LAVENDER AND APRICOT RICE PILAF.. 139
LAVENDER CARAMEL SAUCE 141
HERBES DE PROVENCE 143
CHAPTER 9: CREATING LAVENDER OIL AND ESSENTIAL OIL... 146
   CARRIER OILS... 146
   ESSENTIAL OILS 148
   LAVENDER ESSENTIAL OIL 149
      The Benefits of Lavender Oil *150*
   POTENTIAL SIDE EFFECTS... 152
   DOSAGE AND PREPARATION 152
   WHAT TO LOOK FOR 153
   HOW TO MAKE YOUR OWN LAVENDER OIL................................. 155
   WHICH CARRIER OIL IS BEST?.. 157
   HOW TO MAKE LAVENDER INFUSED OIL..................................... 167
   9 WAYS TO USE LAVENDER OIL.. 168
   VARIOUS LAVENDER OIL BLENDS 170
   GOOD SLEEP BLEND... 170
MASSAGE BLENDS.. 173
   STRESS RELIEF 173
MUSCLE PAIN 175
   PAIN AND COLD RELIEF 177
   BATH SALTS FOR ACHES AND PAINS 178
COSMETIC AND BEAUTY USE 179
   LAVENDER FACIAL STEAM 179
   LAVENDER OIL CONDITIONING SHAMPOO 181
CHAPTER 10: LAVENDER SCENTED GIFTS 184
   LAVENDER BATH BOMBS 185
LAVENDER INFUSED OIL 189

- Lavender Salve 191
- Lavender and Honey Hand Scrub 193
- Lavender Oatmeal Bath Tea 194
- Lavender Mist for Yoga/Exercise Mats 197
- Lavender Bath Salts 198
- Lavender Diffuser Necklace 199
- Lavender Dream Sachet 200
- Lavender Potpourri 202
- Whipped Lavender Body Butter 204

CONCLUSION 206

HERE'S ANOTHER BOOK BY DION ROSSER THAT YOU MIGHT LIKE 207

REFERENCES 208

Introduction

Lavender is one of the heavenliest smells in the world. A garden filled with lavender plants is an incredibly soothing place to be, a haven for bees, and stunning to view. These days, we do more than just grow lavender as a pretty plant in the garden, though. We use it for cooking, body lotions, bath salts, teas, and making crafts such as lavender wands with it. We can also use it to help us sleep, ease anxiety, and even keep the insects away from us.

Lavender is versatile and is easy to grow. Caring for it takes a little work, but, as you will discover, it is one of the most rewarding plants in the world to grow and is worthy of attention.

Sure, there are hundreds of books on the market about growing lavender, so why is this one so different? Why is this the book you should buy?

It's simple – this guide is written in a way that anyone can understand. The information is complex yet easy to digest. It is a hands-on book, with step-by-step instructions on everything, and is perfect for the complete beginner or those with a little more experience who want some new ideas.

I'm not going into any detail here – what I want you to do is turn these pages and start your incredible journey in learning all about lavender and everything you can do with it. Let's go.

Chapter 1: An Introduction to Lavender

Lavandula, commonly known as lavender, is a genus containing 47 species in the Lamiaceae family and – believe it or not – the mint family.

The use of lavender has been documented for the last 2500 years or more. It was used in ancient Egypt in perfume and for mummification. The Romans used it for bathing, cooking, and scenting the air, and in soaps – no surprise, given that the name comes from a Latin verb, "lavare." The Romans also carried lavender with them everywhere through the Roman Empire.

Renaissance and Medieval French women who took in other people's washing were called "lavenders" because they washed the clothes in lavender and laid them on lavender bushes to dry.

Lavender was also used to perfume the air, scent clothes, heal wounds and keep infections away – the Romans also recognized lavender for its healing and antiseptic qualities.

The Ancient Greeks called it "Nardus," after Naarda, a Syrian city, and often shortened it to just Nard. It was a holy herb used to prepare the Holy Essence and is also mentioned in the Bible under its alternative name of "spikenard." It can be found in the Song of Solomon and John, Chapter 12, which mentions that Mary was alleged to have anointed Jesus's feet with "ointment of spikenard" and used her hair to wipe his feet. Jesus decreed that the ointment could not be sold and must be retained for the day he was buried.

In 16th century France, glove makers escaped cholera because they were licensed to use lavender to perfume their wares. In London, lavender was used as one of the apparent remedies against the Great Plague in the 17th century. During the Great Plague, grave robbers were said to have washed in lavender after robbing the graves to avoid getting infected by the plague. In England, Queen Elizabeth I insisted that lavender conserves should be at the royal table and that her residence should have fresh lavender flowers throughout. In 19th century England, Queen Victoria became interested in lavender, leading to an explosion in the popularity of English lavender. Victorians grew lavender in their gardens, and Queen Victoria and Elizabeth both used products from Yardley's of London. And the streets were full of peddlers, selling lavender in bunches to protect people against bad luck.

In Portugal and Spain, people would scatter lavender across church floors or throw it into fires on St John's day in a bid to ward off evil spirits.

Dioscorides was a Greek physician for the Roman army. He wrote that if lavender were ingested, it would help relieve headaches, sore throats, and indigestion, as well as helping clean external wounds.

An English herbalist from the 16th century called John Parkinson wrote that lavender could heal "paines and griefes of the brain and head." At the same time, the French King, Charles VI, insisted on lavender being placed in his pillow to help him sleep. This practice continues to this day.

Traditional Asian medicine has long used lavender for cooling the heart and mind and helping in relaxation. And, more recently, a 1930's French chemist called Rene-Maurice Gattefosse brought lavender to the forefront as a skin healer. He burned his hand and applied lavender oil to it quickly. Impressed by how quickly it healed, he published "Aromatherapie: Les Huiles Essentiales, Hormones Vegetales" and was the first to coin "aromatherapy" as a common phrase we hear today.

During WWII, Margeurite Maury, a French Biochemist, developed a way of applying oils through massage, which is now widely used worldwide.

As lavender became all the rage across Europe, it slowly spread to the Americas, and history claims that the first commercial lavender was grown by the Shakers. On arriving in America from England, they successfully developed herb farms, producing medicines and products, and sold them to distant markets.

Today, we can see commercial cultivations of lavender in England, France, Australia, Italy, the USA, New Zealand, and Canada, to name just a few. In Provence, in the South of France, lavender flowers bloom in late June, filling the air and the markets with the wonderfully heady scent, and craft fairs and flower festivals are full of lavender plants and products.

Practical, Therapeutic, and Medicinal Uses of Lavender

Today, we can see huge fields of lavender, commercially grown not just for the flowers but to extract oil through a process of distillation.

Lavender oil is used as an antiseptic, disinfectant, anti-inflammatory, and in aromatherapy. Many claim that lavender infusions help soothe insect bites and hasten their healing. It can also help heal sunburn, other minor burns, acne, anti-inflammatory conditions, and small cuts. Lavender oils are used in internal fusions, helping to heal indigestion, heartburn, and other conditions. When applied to your temples, some also say that lavender oil can help relieve migraines, headaches, motion sickness and help with relaxation and sleep.

More often than not, sachets are filled with dried lavender flowers to help keep closets, drawers, and linens fresh. It is used in air fresheners to keep any room smelling good, and dried flowers are also now popular as wedding decorations, to make gifts, and as confetti.

Lavender oil is one of the most popular essential oils, extracted from the flowers and, in a small part, from the plant foliage. It can be taken topically, orally, or inhaled. It offers numerous benefits for the skin, including helping eliminate acne, lightening the skin, and reducing dreaded wrinkles. Here are some of the best ways that lavender oil can benefit you:

Acne

Lavender has antiseptic and anti-inflammatory properties, helping to kill off bacteria. This helps heal acne and prevent further outbreaks. When applied to the skin, it helps to open and clean out the pores and reduces inflammation.

For acne treatment, lavender oil should be diluted in a carrier oil such as coconut oil and applied to the skin after washing.

If you mix a couple of drops of lavender oil with a teaspoon of witch hazel, you can also use it as a daily skin toner. Simply soak a ball of cotton wool in it and run it gently over your face. For acne or pimples that prove stubborn, you can add a drop of lavender oil to a drop of argan oil and apply it directly to the spot twice a day.

Dry Skin and Eczema

Dry skin can appear anywhere on the body, and eczema causes itchy, dry, scaly patches. It can be mild or chronic, and it can appear in one place or many. Because lavender also has antifungal properties, it can help soothe eczema and keep it away.

It is also used in treating psoriasis, helping to cleanse the skin and reduce irritation and redness.

To use it, add two drops of lavender oil to two drops of tea tree oil and two teaspoons of coconut oil. Apply it directly to the affected areas twice a day.

Skin Lightening

Because lavender oil has anti-inflammatory properties, it can help lighten your skin. It is used to reduce dark spots, discoloration, redness, and skin blotches, and it may also help with hyperpigmentation.

Face Wrinkles

One thing responsible for facial wrinkles and lines is those pesky free radicals. Lavender oil is packed with antioxidants that fight against these. Using it on wrinkles and as a daily moisturizer is as simple as mixing a few drops with coconut oil and massaging it into your skin.

Anti-Inflammatory Use

Inflammation is painful, and lavender oil is one way to treat it. Because it contains numbing and pain relief properties, it soothes inflammation and, thanks to beta-caryophyllene, it is a natural anti-inflammatory agent. Using it on inflamed burns requires one to three drops mixed with one or two teaspoons of coconut or moringa oil. It can be directly applied to the area up to three times a day.

On sunburn, lavender oil sprays can help relieve the inflammation. Combine 10 to 12 drops of lavender and jojoba oil with two tablespoons of distilled water and a quarter of a cup of aloe vera juice. Shake well and decant into a spray bottle. Spray it up to three times per day on the affected area until it has healed up.

Wound-Healing Use

If you cut or wound yourself, lavender oil can help hasten healing, and lots of studies have confirmed that it has properties that promote tissue healing. Mix a few drops of lavender oil with a few drops of tamanu or coconut oil and use a cotton wool ball or pad to apply it to the wound. Once the wound has healed, you can continue using it to help reduce scarring.

Insect Repellent

Lavender oil works in two ways against irritating insect bites. First, it can repel them, and second, if you do get bitten, it can relieve the irritation and itching. If you check out the ingredients in commercial mosquito repellants, you will see lavender oil listed.

There are several ways to use lavender against insects. First, you can use sprays and candles. Add seven drops of lavender oil to a candle and place it outdoors, especially where you are seated. To make a spray, add four drops of lavender oil to eight ounces of distilled water in a spray bottle. Shake well and spray it over your clothes and body before you go outdoors. You can also plant lavender in areas where you want to repel insects.

Lavender oil helps reduce pain, inflammation, itching, and redness caused by insect bites. It kills off the bacteria in infected bites and relieves the pain and inflammation associated with the infection. Add one or two drops of lavender oil to a carrier oil, such as coconut, and apply to the affected areas twice a day. If the bite stings, add a drop of peppermint oil to the mixture to numb the area.

You can also use lavender oil on poison ivy rashes.

How to Use Lavender Oil for Your Skin

The way lavender oil is used depends on the condition you are treating. It can be used on your skin with a carrier oil or without, although we recommend using one. If you are applying it to an area of your skin that is damaged in some way, use a cotton ball or pad to apply it - that's cleaner than using your fingers, no matter how thoroughly you wash your hands first. And if you are applying to dry skin or wrinkles, you can use your hands to apply the oil directly.

You can also ingest lavender oil in the form of a pill or inhale it through steam in aromatherapy. However, while it is one of the safest oils, it won't suit everyone and can cause some discomfort. If you do have adverse effects from using the oil, such as a rash, stop using it immediately.

Culinary Uses

Because lavender is from the mint family, it has long been used in food preparation, on its own, or as an Herbes de Provence ingredient.

When added to soups, salad, meat, seafood, cheeses, confectionery, desserts, and baked goods, lavender imparts a floral flavor, very elegant and just a little sweet. Most of the time, we use the dried flowers in cooking, although the leaves can be used for some things. The essential oil is only found in the flowers or buds, where the flavor and scent originate.

No matter how you use lavender in food, it goes way beyond its scent to provide a delicate yet rich flavor, and the only limit to the recipes you can use it in is your imagination.

Cooking with Lavender Tips

When cooking with lavender, you can use fresh or dried flowers but, if you choose dried, only use one-third of the amount compared to fresh flowers as dried flowers are much stronger in taste and scent.

The real key is to experiment – start small and add more to taste. If you add too much, your food will taste bitter and smell strongly of perfume. Lavender is quite strong, and a little bit goes quite a long way.

The lavender flowers add excellent color to salads. In many recipes, especially bread, lavender is a perfect substitute for rosemary. You can add the flowers to sugar, seal them in a jar for a couple of weeks and then use the sugar in cakes and other baked sweet goods, or custards and sweet sauces. You can use a coffee grinder or a mortar and pestle to grind the buds and, if you want to retain the stems, they make great substitutes for skewers in fruit or shrimp kabobs.

The flowers look lovely in a glass of sparkling wine or champagne, and they taste great too. You can add them to chocolate cake or use them to garnish ice cream or sorbet. You can use it in soups, stews, sauces, sorbets, custard, and so on. Later in the book, we'll be devoting an entire chapter to cooking with lavender and offering some fantastic recipes for you to try.

WARNING

Never eat the flowers you get from garden centers, garden nurseries, or florists. Most of the time, the plant has been sprayed with pesticides and is not suitable for food crops!

Chapter 2: Different Types of Lavender

Lavender is one of the most popular flowering herbs, belonging to the mint family and dating at least 2500 years back. It has many uses, not just as a flower in the garden but also in the household, beauty, cleansing, therapeutic, and medicinal areas. It is also one of the best plants to repel many insects, including the dreaded mosquito.

The mint family is home to over 200 genera and includes over 5000 species, including basil, thyme, rosemary, and lavender. For this reason, the lavender leaves and flowers are edible, whether they are dried or fresh.

The big problem many people face is which type of lavender to grow. There are hundreds of variants, around 450 to be precise, grouped into 45 species. No doubt, there are more that haven't yet been discovered, including hybrids, but most people find that the following 12 types are the most accessible and the easiest to grow and use.

French Lavender (Lavandula Dentata)

French lavender is delicate, with less of a heady fragrance and color than most other lavender species. However, the blooms are the longest-lasting of all lavenders, lasting through summer and climate allowing, well into the fall. It is a large variety and can grow around two feet in both height and width. However, French lavender will not tolerate extremes of temperature.

French Lavender likes warm climates, full sun, and sandy soil. Once established, it needs little water and is suited to hardiness zones 8 and 9.

Ballerina (Lavandula Stoechas)

Another French lavender, oddly named "Spanish Lavender Ballerina," blooms with white flowers. As the plant matures, the flowers fade into a pink and then purple color. The plant prefers milder summer and winter climates and will flower in May, blooming again in June and then again in late summer/early fall.

It prefers full sun and, once established, needs little water. It grows best in sandy soil and is suitable for hardiness zones 8 and 9.

Kew Red (Lavender Stoechas)

Kew Red is another French lavender species named after its flower coloring – crimson-violet with pale pink top petals. It has one of the longest flowering seasons, running from late spring through to the fall, and in milder climates, you can see the flowers all year round.

It prefers milder winters and summers, grows well in sandy soil in full sun, and once established, it needs little water. It is suitable for hardiness zones 7, 8, and 9.

Anouk (Lavender Stoechas)

An early bloomer, Anouk can be seen flowering much earlier than most French lavenders, beginning in early to mid-spring. The heads are deep purple and plump, with pale purple petals.

It can withstand hotter summers than many other lavenders, prefers to grow in full sun, and likes mild winters. It is drought-resistant, so water requirements are low, and it suits hardiness zones 6, 7, 8, 9, and 10.

Betty's Blue (Lavandula Angustifolia)

An English lavender, the large flowers are a deep violet-blue on compact plants shaped like domes. It has a sweet fragrance and will bloom just once in the season, in mid-summer. Because this has such fragrant flowers, they are usually used in potpourris after being dried.

Betty's Blue prefers mild summer and winter climates and grows best in sandy soil in full sun. Water requirements are low once established, and it suits hardiness zones 5, 6, 7, 8, and 9.

Lavenite Petite (Lavandula Angustifolia)

This is another English lavender with unique, dense, pom-pom-shaped flowers. These flowers are one of the most fragrant and display a light purple that pops off the flower. It blooms mid to late spring and is a great variety for attracting bees and butterflies to their gardens.

Lavenite Petite likes sandy soil in full sun and grows best in climates with warm summers and mild winters. It is suitable for hardiness zones 5, 6, 7, 8, and 9.

Hidcote (Lavandula Angustifolia)

A very popular lavender, Hidcote has beautiful dark purple flowers with contrasting green-blue foliage. The flowers retain their color after drying, making them an excellent choice for making decorations and crafts. The flowers bloom from late spring to early summer, dependent on the climate.

Hidcote prefers sandy soil in full sun and requires little water. It likes warmer climates and is suitable for hardiness zones 5, 6, 7, 8, and 9.

Impress Purple (Lavandula x Intermedia)

Impress purple is a hybrid lavender, popular in flower bouquets because of its long dark purple flowers. These are the richest colors on any lavender, and the trick to ensure blooming is long-lasting is to remove any faded flowers. Flowers appear from mid-summer through to late summer and give off a heady fragrance.

Impress Purple likes sandy soils, full sun, and requires little water once established. It prefers hotter summers and warmer winters and is suitable for hardiness zones 6, 7, and 8.

Hidcote Giant (Lavandula x Intermedia)

Another hybrid, the Hidcote Giant, has pale violet flowers that spread wonderfully on long stems. It has won awards for its beauty and its fragrance. Used in bouquets, it blooms from mid to late summer and is another wonderful lavender for those who want bees and butterflies in their gardens.

Hidcote Giant likes full sun, sandy soils and requires little water. It prefers milder climates where summers and winters are warm and is suitable for hardiness zones 5, 6, 7, and 8.

Grosso (Lavandula x Intermedia)

A hybrid variety, Grosso stands at around two feet tall with fragrant narrow leaves topped with dark purple flowers. Grosso can withstand colder winters down to 15°F, and provided they are pruned as soon as flowering finishes, they can last for a long time. Grosso is one of the varieties grown for extracting lavender oil.

Grosso prefers mild summers and can tolerate colder winters. It likes sandy soil, lots of sun, and needs little water. Grosso is suitable for hardiness zones 5, 6, 7, and 8.

Portuguese Lavender (Lavandula Latifola)

Portuguese lavender goes by a more common name of spike lavender. Its flowers are simple and elegant, producing bulbs of pale lilac along the stems. It is more commonly used as culinary lavender; it is a natural magnet for the bees and butterflies with fragrant, sweet leave.

It prefers warmer climates with mild winters, like sandy soil and full sun. It requires little water and is suitable for hardiness zones 5, 6, 7, 8, and 9.

Egyptian Lavender (Lavandula Multifida)

Another name for Egyptian lavender is Fern-Leaf because its leaves are bipinnate and furry. It smells different from other lavenders, not quite so sweet, and, once established, it can be left to its own devices if it is in well-drained soil and has sufficient room to grow. Egyptian lavender flowers appear in late spring.

Egyptian lavender likes sandy soil, a lot of sun, and little water. It prefers to grow in mild climates and is suitable for hardiness zones 8, 9, 10, and 11.

The Best Lavender for You

When choosing which type of lavender to grow in your garden, the first consideration is your climate. Second, you must consider each of the four main types of lavender to decide which ones provide what you want.

The four main groups are:

English Lavender

Suits hardiness zones 5, 6, 7, and 8

English lavender displays small clusters of flowers, blooming early in the season, with green-blue leaves. It is a good performing type for Northern areas and can overwinter to zone 5. In colder zones, gardeners will need to create warmer microclimates in their lavender beds to ensure the plant can survive.

A fragrant species, English Lavender is typically used as culinary lavender.

Lavandin Hybrids

Suits hardiness zones 5, 6, 7, 8, 9, and 10

English lavender hybrids flower later than other species and are higher in essential oils. Their leaves are typically large and green-gray, and they are well known for growing fast and have a strong-smelling fragrance.

This group includes some of the more popular species, such as Grosso, Provence, and Phenomenal.

French Lavender

Suits hardiness zones 5, 6, 7, 8, 9, and 10

French lavenders prefer much milder climates with warmer winters and don't do well in harsh winters. They are ornamental, with needle-like leaves with teeth - hence the name, Dentata. They don't have a strong fragrance as the English varieties and grow well in rockeries and containers. They look lovely when planted in rows beside walkways and paths. French lavender likes gritty soil with lots of sun.

Spanish Lavender

Suits hardiness zones 7, 8, 9, and 10

Spanish lavender has large flowers, displaying petals shaped like pinecones at the top and silvery leaves. They have a fragrance much like eucalyptus and can tolerate humid climates than many other varieties. They are popular in small gardens and courtyards, creating a stunning focal point, and grow well in containers. They can easily withstand stylized pruning.

What Lavender Can Do for You

Now you know the types of lavender suited to your zone, it's time to consider what you want from your lavender. Different lavender species have different uses, so consider what you want before deciding on your lavender plants.

Best Lavender for Perennial Gardens

If your perennial garden has plenty of sun, any type of lavender will do well. The only requirement is fast-draining soil, and that other plants in the same bed must have the same low water needs. Do NOT plant lavender in beds with other plants that need a lot of water as your lavender will not thrive.

The short varieties look much better when placed at the front of a border or along walkways.

Best Lavender for Humid, Hot Climates

Most lavenders do not particularly like humid and hot weather, and many Southern gardeners have found it very hard to grow it successfully. In fact, the only way to grow it in the south is to create cool microclimates. However, there is a new lavender that will grow very well in southern summers.

It's called Phenomenal and is a true English lavender. It has been well tested from Texas through Georgia and has even been shown to grow well in Florida. Spanish lavender also grows better in humid and hot climates, so consider Silver Anouk or Anouk varieties. The main point is to plant in well-draining soil or ensure that you let the soil dry out between watering - this is important when you plant in containers.

Best Cold-Hardy Lavender

Look at an established lavender, and you will see it is semi-woody. A perennial plant, lavender is evergreen in warmer climates while, in colder climates, the plants will die back. This means their green color disappears during the winter and may return the following year - or it may not.

The best varieties for colder climates are Hidcote and Munstead; both are less likely to die back in zone 5 climates. Phenomenal is also an excellent choice; it tolerates humid climates won't die back completely in cold climates.

Tip - in colder climates, wait until winter is over before you prune lavender so you can see the extent of the damage that winter has done.

Best Compact Lavender Plants

Lavender prefers a full sun location in good draining soil. That makes them perfect for rockeries and ideal for planting alongside small perennials and succulents to heighten the bed. The best varieties are Thumbelina Leigh and Blue Cushion, both varieties of English lavender.

Best Fragrant Lavender for Drying and Preserving

Perhaps the best lavender for this is Provence, a hybrid lavender with a high level of essential oil. This is the most frequently used variety in products with a lavender scent, such as potpourri, sachets, soap, etc. Blooming in mid to late summer, this is best harvested first thing in the morning, when bottom flowers begin opening. The bundles should be tied tightly and hung upside down to dry somewhere cool and dry.

Alongside Provence, Vera and Grosso varieties are also good choices.

Best Lavender for Containers

One of the biggest concerns of gardeners who choose to grow lavender in containers is interest. Most people want unusual plants, great colors that "pop," large flowers, and plants that behave reasonably well. One of the best lavender varieties, ticking every box, is Goodwin Creek Grey, a compact fragrant plant with deep purple blooms and contrasting grey leaves.

This variety grows well on its own in containers, or it could be paired with another drought-tolerant herb such as creeping thyme. Other great varieties include Mini Blue, SuperBlue, Silver Anouk, Anouk, and Thumbelina Leigh.

Best Lavenders for Pollinator Gardens

To be fair, all lavender is excellent for this because pollinators of all types will flock to them. Plant your favorite lavenders near or beside other flowers that attract pollinators, such as Echinacea. Some of the best lavender varieties that pollinators absolutely love are Phenomenal, Pastor's Pride, and SuperBlue. Choose English lavender varieties where possible, as they tend to attract more pollinators than other varieties.

Best Lavender For Topiaries

Topiaries require a great deal of patience, but one of the best-looking topiaries of all are herbs. Anouk, a Spanish lavender with large flowers, looks marvelous when clipped into a shape and will bloom throughout the summer. You can also train and clip Silver Anouk.

The Best Lavender for Hedges and Knot Gardens

Knot gardens look better with contrasting foliage, more so in the winter when many other flowers have died back. Keeping knot gardens tidy involves plants that can be sheared -shaped through leaf trimming.

One of the best French lavenders for this is Goodwin Creek Gray, with its stunning silver foliage. While it flowers all summer, this won't be a major concern to those who want tight hedges. However, some people prefer to allow it to bloom and then trim it into shape. Some of the best choices are Vera, Pastor's Pride, and Royal Velvet.

Best Culinary Lavender

The English lavenders are the best for cooking and can be found in Herbes de Provence, with thyme, savory, rosemary, oregano, and marjoram. This can be used for spicing up grilled meats, potatoes, and roasted vegetables – later, I will give you the recipe to make your own Herbes de Provence.

Some of the best varieties include Munstead, Hidcote, and Blue Cushion.

Do be careful that you don't spray pesticides on or near culinary lavender plants.

Chapter 3: How to Plant Lavender and Care For it

Lavender doesn't require a great deal of attention once you have planted it and it has become established. Once you have determined the varieties you want, it's time to think about planting it. If you are still undecided, remember that lavender is pretty drought tolerant and is easy to upkeep. Additionally, its strong fragrance helps deter unwanted pests from your garden, and it attracts vast numbers of pollinators to your garden.

Choosing Plants by Zone

To be honest, lavender is not a challenging plant whether the gardener has years of experience or is just starting out. However, specific guidelines must be adhered to when you grow lavender, four to be precise:

- Lavender loves the heat and sun
- Lavender hates water
- Lavender requires space to grow
- Lavender requires lean, well-drained soil.

This is understandable when you consider that lavender originated from arid and hot climates, like France, Italy, and Spain.

If you don't compensate for the climate, your lavender will not do very well at best, and, at worst, it will die.

Southern Climates

Gardeners who live in southern regions with long, hot summers must provide some shade during the height of the day when the sun is at its hottest. They must also ensure plants are well-spaced to allow for good air circulation.

If your region is quite humid, your plants need serious space between them to prevent diseases from spreading and ensuring the maximum amount of airflow.

Remember that lavender hates water, so you must ensure the soil is well-drained and use lots of stone mulch that dries quickly.

In these regions, the French or Spanish lavenders are the best options as they thrive well in steamy, hot conditions.

Northern Climates

If you live in the more northern regions, cold weather is a given, along with longer winters and wet, soggy soil. While northern areas are somewhat more challenging to grow lavender, it can be achieved with a little patience and time. Many growers will use containers for their lavender and bring them indoors during the colder months.

One of the best species is English lavender and is one of the more cold-hardy hybrid plants.

Many lavender varieties will thrive only in certain conditions, so knowing your zone and weather temperament is the first step to success. Once you understand your climate, you can choose a suitable species.

Growing Your Lavender Outdoors

Now it's time to plant your lavender. If you have planted in the ground outdoors, this section will walk you through the process step-by-step.

When to Plant

If you live in a northern climate and want to plant your lavender early, skip this section and head to the section on growing in containers. Alternatively, you could wait until after the last frost has passed before planting your lavender outdoors, so long as spring is not too wet.

When the weather is wet, planting lavender outside is a challenge, but it does provide the plant with sufficient time to strengthen and become acclimatized before the winter arrives.

Don't forget that you should really plant lavender in containers if you have long, harsh, wet winters. That way, you can bring it indoors – in the house, greenhouse, or a polytunnel – for the coldest months.

In southern climates, where the winters are not long and harsh, the best time to plant is in November.

Where to Plant

Lavender requires plenty of space for sufficient airflow, especially in humid climates, so consider this when choosing your planting spot.

One rule of thumb to follow is to space them as far apart as the height they grow. So, if your chosen variety grows around two feet tall, each plant should be spaced about two feet apart. The southern varieties are much stronger than the northern ones and grow much taller. Colder weather makes the plants stay short and dense as a mechanism of protecting themselves against the weather.

If your region has slightly cold winters, you can implement a couple of tricks to create a natural temperature increase around the plants. First, stone walls that face south or building walls tend to radiate heat and keep your plants warmer, so consider that as a planting spot.

You can also add stone mulch around your plants to increase the heat – the more heat, the better the plant will thrive.

Drainage is another consideration when deciding where to plant your lavender, especially when you get an average of 12 to 15 inches of rainfall. Lavender will not survive in soggy soil, so look for an area in your garden where the soil drains well. If not, think about adding organic amendments to your soil. Some things you can add are perlite, sand, good compost, mulch, or vermiculite.

Alternatively, plant your lavender in raised beds where you can control the soil and water levels.

How to Plant Your Lavender

So, now you know how the cold and rain affects your plants, it's time to look at another critical component – soil.

If you want happy plants that thrive, you'll need lean, alkaline soil. If your soil is acidic, you can change it to alkaline. Test your soil using a tester you can purchase from any garden center or online:

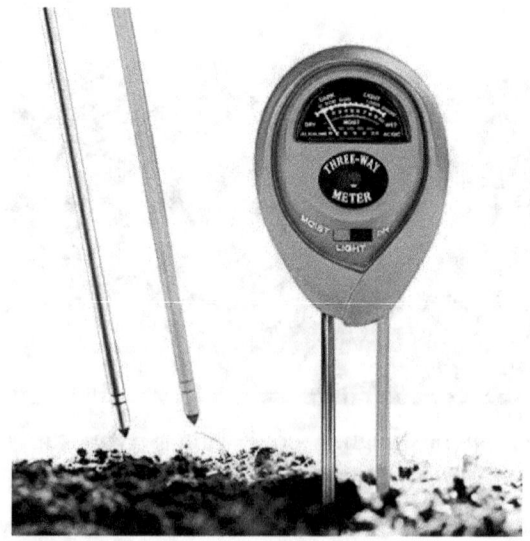

If it shows as acidic, add half a cup of a mixture of bone meal and lime to the hole you are planting your lavender in. Every year, add the same mixture to the soil, and your lavender will thank you for it with strong growth.

Lavender reaches its peak in its third growth year. After two or three years, if your plants are not doing what you expect, test the soil. At this stage, if the soil is too acidic, add some crushed oyster shells to make it more alkaline.

Another requirement is to ensure your soil is dry enough for the lavender to grow. If you are worried that your soil will get too wet, dig the hole six inches deeper than the root bulb and add a layer of gravel to it. Fill the hole in and mound it between 12 and 24 inches above the soil line before planting the lavender. Yes, it seems like a big mound, but this will do two things where your soil doesn't drain very well. First, it will provide the plant with the maximum amount of drainage, and second, it provides much better air circulation around the plants.

Last, choose a spot that gets at least six hours of sunlight per day.

Choosing and Preparing Your Planting Site

In terms of soil quality, lavender will thrive in soil that is poor to moderately fertile. Where your soil is clay or compacted hard, dig in some organic matter to give it better drainage.

Let's get planting.

Step One

Choose young lavender plants that are strong and vigorous and set them in an open, sunny area with plenty of air circulation, about 12 to 18 inches apart for dwarf varieties and 24 to 36 inches apart for the larger varieties.

Step Two

Check that your soil's pH is between 6.7 and 7.3. If it is more acidic, dig in some lime and bone meal to bring it up to alkaline. Increase drainage by digging in some sharp builder's sand before you plant. Alternatives to growing in the ground include raised beds, at the top of a slope, or along walls, where you can control the soil, and the drainage is much better.

If you are planting your lavender in perennial or herb beds, create mounds to plant the lavender in.

Step Three

Dig the holes and place your lavender plants in them. The hole should be twice the depth and width of the plant's root ball. When you remove the plants from the pots, if the roots are clinging to the sides, rough them up a little to encourage them to grow outward.

Step Four

Plant the lavender in the hole, ensuring the top of the root ball lines up with the soil line. Fill the hole around the plant and press the soil firmly down.

Step Five

Water the plants thoroughly. This will compress the soil and get rid of any air pockets. From now on, your plants will only need watering if the ground goes very dry.

Caring for Your Lavender

Lavender doesn't need a great deal of care, but you need to do a few things, especially when you first plant your plants.

Water

The most common cause of lavender plants dying is over-watering. With the humble lavender, less really is more, so if you take away nothing else from this guide, *make sure that you don't drown your plants!*

Lavender is drought tolerant, which means it prefers its soil to be dry. But here's the kick - you can't let it dry out completely.

If you don't know how often you should be watering your lavender, here's a tip - water it deeply and then wait for the soil to dry before you water it again. That pH tester you bought to test the soil should be a 3-1. It will test for soil pH, moisture content, and light levels and is one of the handiest tools you will ever use in your garden.

Sun

Lavender plants love the sun, so plant yours in a sunny place - at least 6 hours per day is best. However, if you live in a hot climate, there can be some shade but not too much - lavender won't bloom well if it doesn't get enough light.

Fertilizer

This section is added to tell you that you *need not know anything about fertilizer* because lavender simply doesn't need it. In fact, the more fertilizer is in your soil, the worse the plant will grow. You can add compost to bad garden soil every one or two years, but it isn't a requirement. I have lavender growing in my garden that is quite neglected, and it hasn't suffered one bit.

Mulch

Mulch isn't necessary because lavender doesn't need the moisture to be kept in the soil. However, you can use it if you want; just use small bark or gravel and don't push it right up against the plant crown - leave a few inches clear, or you may encourage too much moisture, and the roots will rot. If you use sand or light-colored mulch, it helps keep the plant and the soil warm and helps with drainage.

Trimming and Pruning

In the summer, you can harvest the stalks and use them dried or fresh. However, if you are not growing your lavender for anything other than your garden, you should still deadhead any faded blossoms. This makes the plant look tidier and can help it to flower again.

Plants two years or older should be trimmed back in spring, taking the stems back by about a third. This helps new growth, better foliage, and stunning flowers.

Growing Lavender in Containers

Lavender is perfectly suited to growing in containers. It is the ideal solution for those with little room, have really poor soil, or live in climates where the winters are colder, and the plants need to be protected from the cold.

Here's how to grow your lavender in a container.

Step One

After choosing your lavender variety, you need to pick a container. It must be large as some lavender varieties can grow into bushes. Try to get one about 12 to 16 inches in diameter. Then ensure that it has drainage – one hole of approximately half an inch in the center of the bottom will do the job. Last, add a layer of small gravel to the bottom of the container to help with drainage.

Step Two

Select your soil. It should be sandy soil with good drainage – you can get the right one from your nearest garden center. Fill the container three-quarters of the way up and sift the soil with your hands to break up any lumps. Add one tablespoon of lime and stir it in – this will ensure the soil has the correct alkaline pH.

Step Three

Remove your lavender plant from its pot. Hold the pot and gently squeeze the bottom of it to loosen the lavender plant. Tilt the pot and pull the lavender gently, holding the plant's base. If the soil is sufficiently loose, it should slide right out. The lavender should come out with all its dirt intact around the root ball – you don't want to damage this, so be careful how you handle it.

Step Four

Place the lavender plant in the middle of the container, ensuring that the plant's base is about three inches down from the container's rim. Nestle it into the soil and gently tease the root ball to allow some of the roots to escape. This will encourage the roots to grow out. Typically, when you buy plants in small pots, they will be somewhat root-bound because they've been in the pot for too long, and the roots are fighting the soil for space. The soil will be hard and compact and, if you don't tease out the roots, they won't expand, thus killing the plant. This won't be the case with all plants but loosening the soil is always a good idea.

Now add more soil to the container to fill it, gently patting the soil down. Do NOT compact it, or the water won't drain through. The crown of your lavender plant should be approximately one inch above the soil line.

Step Five

Water your lavender plant thoroughly. Make it a good watering because you won't be doing it again for at least a week.

Step Six

Add some mulch. It should be about two inches thick and made from pea gravel or small bark. This not only helps with drainage and prevents root rot from setting in, but it can also help keep the soil warm. Using light-colored mulch helps, as it reflects the sun's light and heat back to the plant.

Step Seven

Place your container where it can get at least six hours of sun per day. If you keep it in the shade, it will not grow properly, nor will the flowers have that wonderful fragrance. However, do keep it sheltered from the wind as strong winds can damage the plants.

Caring for Lavender in Containers

When it is established, lavender rarely needs a lot of watering. However, when you grow it in containers, it will need more water than if it were planted in the ground. Wait until the soil in the pot is dry, and then drench it thoroughly until you see water running out of the bottom of the pot. This means it is sufficiently wet.

Last, if your climate is colder in the winter, take your potted plants indoors for the colder months. In your house, a garage, greenhouse, etc., will do so long as they cannot get the frost or cold winds on them. You can also consider wrapping light garden fleece around the container and plant. You won't need to worry too much about water - simply lift the pot and, if it feels light or the plants are beginning to wilt, then you can water it a little.

Chapter 4: Lavender Diseases and Pests

Lavender is one of the most beautiful plants you can add to your garden, stunning to look at when in full bloom and emitting a heady fragrance. Like all plants, a few diseases and pests may attack your lavender plants; although, to be fair, unlike some plants, lavender doesn't attract too many. However, there are a couple of things you need to look out for.

Spittlebugs

Commonly called froghoppers, spittlebugs are one of the most common pests to attack lavender. They are more noticeable in the spring months because you will see a foamy substance, much like spittle, on your plants. This looks nasty, but you will rarely find these bugs at a high enough level to be classified as an infestation that will harm your plants. Occasionally though, the stems with the spittle on them will die, and that makes your plants look unattractive.

How to Control Spittlebugs

Usually, you don't need chemicals or pesticides to treat spittlebug. The easiest way to control is to use your hose and squirt a strong spray of water at them – this knocks the bug and spittle off the plant.

Whiteflies

Lavender is just one of many plants that whiteflies are attracted to. They feed on the sap and, although they will not kill the plant, they can cause ugly damage. Whiteflies are small insects, powdery-looking, and you will find them in the undersides of the lavender leaves; a few won't do much damage, but heavy infestations can cause your plant growth to slow and the foliage to become mottled and yellow. Whiteflies also leave a honeydew behind that can cause sooty mold.

How to Control Whiteflies

If you have large populations, control is difficult because no readily available pesticides will do the job effectively. You can purchase natural enemies commercially, such as a predatory ladybird beetle called Delphastus pusillus, which feed on whitefly at all stages. However, control methods like this should be used in conjunction with other types of biological controls. Another way to remove them is to handpick the whitefly off your plants, and using a strong stream of water from a hose can also remove them.

You also apply a layer of reflective mulch or even aluminum foil around the base of the plants – these may also help repel other pests too, such as aphids.

Aphids

The aphid is not a harmful insect on its own, but it can spread something called alfalfa mosaic disease, which is common to lavender. If your plants are diseased, the symptoms will show as yellow patches on the shoots and leaves, and, occasionally, you may see the foliage twist. Typically, this won't kill the plants, but it can slow down growth and stop the plant from blooming. If your plants are affected, the only thing you can do is remove the plant in its entirety and burn it to stop it from spreading to other plants.

How to Prevent Alfalfa Mosaic Virus

Preventing alfalfa mosaic disease requires that you control the aphid population. Also, ensure your gardening tools are cleaned and sterilized to stop the disease from spreading – as it will attack other plants. Some horticultural oils and insecticides can help, but you need to know these will also destroy beneficial insects and natural predators. The best thing to do is prune off any sections of the surrounding plants with aphid infestations and use reflective mulch or aluminum foil around your lavender.

Root Rot

Because lavender is native to arid, hot regions, like the Mediterranean, they prefer hot, sunny, and dry areas. Root rot is one of the fungal diseases that live in heavy, wet soil. Infected plants will start wilting and turning brown, and the best way to deal with it is to cut out infected plant sections and roots and destroy them. When you do water your lavender, do it first thing in the morning, and don't wet the leaves. This is where soaker hoses are the best - simply lay it along the base of the plants and deeply water it once a week. The soaker hose will send the water into the soil and not all over the foliage. Leave the soil to dry out before you water again - lavender prefers drier soil.

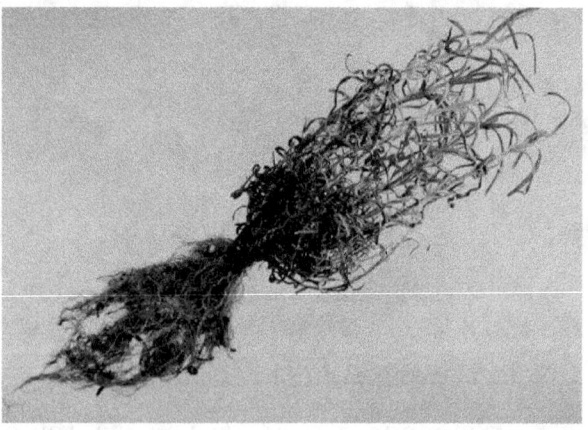

Lavender Shab

Lavender Shab is a fungal spore that attacks lavender plants, causing the stems to turn brown and twist. You will also see small black spots on the plant stems. Infected plants should be removed and destroyed – burn them. Do NOT place them in your compost pile; otherwise, the disease will remain prevalent.

Companion Planting

One of the best ways to keep pests away from your lavender is to employ an age-old, time-tested method of companion planting. Gardeners and farmers have long employed this to attract the good insects, deter the bad ones, and help stimulate plant growth.

Some companion plants help others grow, while some will grow better if planted next to a specific crop. Here are some jobs companion plants do in the garden:

1. They repel pests - Lots of pests can invade gardens, especially vegetable gardens - cucumber beetles, cabbage worms, Mexican bean beetles, cabbage moths, carrot flies - the list goes on. Many companion plants, such as catnip, rue, and marigolds, repel certain pests and should be strategically planted to keep certain crops free of pests.

2. They attract beneficial insects - The right plants attract pollinators like bees and natural predators like ladybirds. These need some encouragement and, to help them, many gardeners plant borage.

3. They improve nutrients in the soil - Any crop will take valuable nutrients, which leaves the gardener with a lot of work to do before the start of the next season in renewing those nutrients. However, some companion plants, such as pole and bush beans, add nitrogen and other nutrients into the soil, helping to keep other plants strong and healthy. A tip - if you grow beans and peas in your garden, when you harvest the crops and remove the plants, leave the roots in the ground. This is where nitrogen forms in small nodules - leaving the roots to decompose can help replace this valuable nutrient naturally.

4. They encourage better taste and faster growth - Companion plants like summer savory, chamomile, and marjoram, will release certain chemicals into the air, encouraging faster growth in plants around them and better-tasting produce.

5. They provide ground cover - Plant spreading plants, such as oregano, to cover the soil, keeping it cool for plants that prefer lower temperatures, and keeping weeds under control.

6. They provide shade - Some plants, like asparagus and zucchini, grow tall and leafy, and help protect some sensitive plants from the sun.

7. They act as markers - When you plant slow-growers, it isn't always easy to see the rows before the seeds sprout. Fast-growers, like radishes planted between the slow-growing rows, help you easily see where they are.

Five Companion Plants for Lavender

One of the most common lavender varieties is Lavandula angustifolia or English Lavender, cultivated for lavender oil. Less common varieties, such as Spanish and French lavender, are cultivated mainly for essential oils and potpourri. Lavender, as you know, likes a full sun position, and a lot of companion plants can help keep pests and diseases away and help it grow better. Five of the best are:

1. **Herbs** - As part of the mint family, lavender loves other herbs such as oregano and basil. Both increase the growth and strength of lavender when planted nearby because they can repel different fly species and aphids.

2. **Brassicas** - By planting lavender around the edges of cauliflower, cabbage, and other brassica crops, you can help repel moths and other insects that lay their eggs on the undersides of the leaves.

3.   **Echinacea** - Believe it or not, echinacea hates water even more than lavender does, and it is an excellent plant for attracting pollinators when planted near lavender.

4.   **Alliums** - Alliums give off a strong scent as lavender does, and this scent helps distract and repel pests, making them the perfect companion plants anywhere in the garden.

5.   **Fruit Trees** - Fruit trees need pollination, and lavender attracts bees in their swarms. However, lavender also repels other insects that target fruit trees, such as the codling moth, which attacks apple trees.

How to Revive a Dying Lavender Plant

Lavender really doesn't require a great deal of maintenance, but it can live for up to 15 years when cared for properly. Because they originate in the Mediterranean, they do require a certain set of conditions to thrive.

If you are having problems with your lavender dying, some of those conditions must be replicated, specifically the soil conditions. There are a few ways to revive a dying plant, but you need to know what has caused the lavender to fai

1.

Identify the Problem

Common reasons your lavender may need to be revived are:

- **Root rot** - because the soil is too wet.

- **Leggy lavender** – possibly with yellow leaves, which means the soil is too fertile.

- **Woody growth with few blooms** – a lack of pruning will cause this.

- **Lack of sun** – this causes poor growth because lavender needs at least six hours of sun per day.

- **Planted in the wrong container** – the container should be at least 12 to 16 inches across and must have drainage holes.

So, how do you solve these problems? Luckily, the plant can be brought back to life on most occasions:

Root Rot

- **Symptoms** – the lavender is drooping or wilting, and the foliage has turned yellow or brown.
- **Cause** – overwatering, the soil not draining properly, high humidity levels, plants too close together, or organic material, such as mulch or dropped leaves too close to the plant.

Because the lavender plant originated in sandy, dry Mediterranean coastal areas, it doesn't need too much water. However, it does need to be planted in soil that drains fast, it needs a lot of sun, and it does need airflow.

During the growing season, lavender only needs to be watered once a fortnight and never over the winter months.

How to Revive a Lavender with Root Rot

1. If your lavender shows the signs of this, the first thing to do is stop watering it. If you planted it in a container, move it somewhere sheltered so it can't get any rainfall.

2. Next, clear any dead leaves or other organic material from around the base of the plant. These materials do nothing more than retain the moisture in the ground, promoting the ideal conditions for root rot to thrive.

3. Use a garden fork to loft the lavender carefully from the ground and look at the roots. If there are any that are soft and rotting, snip them off using sterilized pruners.

4. Replant the lavender somewhere new, ensuring full sun and fresh soil. Add gravel or sand to the soil first to ensure it drains well.

As long as you replant it in good draining soil and do NOT water it for at least two weeks, your lavender should revive. Where you have clay or other poor draining soil, it will serve no purpose to replant it - the conditions will ensure that root rot will thrive anywhere where the soil doesn't drain.

If so, you are better off planting the lavender in a large container or a raised bed. These planting options allow you to control the soil and drainage much better, and you can tailor it to the lavender's requirements.

Also, ensure that each lavender is planted two to three feet away from the next one. Airflow is a requirement for keeping moisture away from the plants and helping to dry the soil out.

Follow these steps, and you should see signs of improvement in your lavender within three weeks.

Leggy Lavender with Yellow Foliage

- **Symptoms** – long, leggy stems with few blooms, and the foliage could turn yellow.

• **Causes** – too much nitrogen in the soil, use of fertilizers.

Lavender likes low to moderately fertilized soil, and they naturally grow in gravelly or sandy soils. If you plant them in soil with too much organic content or too many nutrients, your plants will grow leggy, and they won't have many flowers and are likely to turn yellow.

You need not feed lavender, and you need not add fertilizer to the soil – that is why the foliage turns yellow, a sign that the soil has too much nitrogen. This makes your plants more likely to get diseases.

How to Revive Leggy Lavender with Yellow Foliage

1. If you are guilty of fertilizing your lavender plants, stop – NOW.

2. Carefully dig lavender up and transplant it to a pot or somewhere else in your garden, where the soil is not quite so rich. Also, amend the soil using gravel or sand.

3. Prune the leggy parts of the plant in early spring or late in the fall but only cut off a third of the good growth. If you cut it right back to the woody base, it will not rejuvenate as it should.

4. Follow the best practices for lavender plans and be aware that revival may take time – be patient.

Using sand or gravel to amend the soil is very important. It balances soil fertility and reduces it to the levels needed by lavender plants. Neither adds nutrition to the soil, and neither will retain any nutrients to any real levels.

When you plant lavender in a container, the mixture should be 70% compost and 30% gravel or sand. The same goes for amending your borders.

Once your lavender has settled in, full revival may take a season and a decent pruning.

Woody Growth

- **Symptoms** – the lavender looks untidy, has few blooms and the stems are more likely to split as the wood is more vulnerable than new growth, which is more flexible.

- **Causes** – any lavender variety will eventually turn woody the older it gets. However, correct yearly pruning will impede woody growth from the base of the plant.

One of the biggest challenges gardeners face is stopping their lavender from going woody too quickly. Well maintained, English lavender can live for 15 years, but French typically survives only four or five years. Increasing longevity is important and correct pruning can reduce the rate of wood growing from the base.

How to Revive Woody Lavender

Sadly, woody lavender is one of the hardest things to fix, and the only way you can do so is to prune the plant back. However, you shouldn't prune into the wood. Woody growth at the plant's base is not productive and will support no new growth. If you do cut into the woody part, the flowers will not appear, and the plant may die.

The best way to do it is to prune off the top third of any green growth on the plant and, as far as you can, prune the entire plant into the shape of a mound. The best time is March/April or September/October – before flowering or after.

There isn't much else you can do besides pruning it. If the woody growth is too much, it may just be better to pull it up and start again with new plants. One of the most cost-effective ways of doing this is to take a cutting and propagate it. This is easy to do and doesn't require hormone root powder. Early spring is the best time to take cuttings.

How to Revive Lavender in a Container

The most common reasons for unhealthy lavender in containers are:

- The container is too small for insulation or for the roots to grow.
- The container has no drainage holes or drip tray beneath it.

The ideal size for a container is at least 16 inches across and at least the same depth. This size container has sufficient room to allow the roots to be insulated against colder temperatures and to contain the correct mix of soil and sand for good drainage.

If you use small containers, your plant's growth will be inhibited, and water cannot drain quickly away from the roots. If the soil is not porous enough, there will be insufficient oxygen in the soil for root respiration, which will invite diseases.

Also, make sure your containers have drainage holes so the plant roots do not sit in water. One of the worst mistakes is to use a drip dray beneath the pot. People mistakenly think they are doing a good thing, catching any water that runs out, so it doesn't run all over their patio. All that does is keeps the roots wet, thus leading to a very unhappy lavender plant.

Your lavender does not need watering often, so when you do water it, it should be done, so the water runs from the bottom of the pot. Stand your container on that lawn or soil somewhere and leave it for half an hour after you water it, allowing the water to run out and not run all over your patio.

How to Revive Shaded Lavender

Every species of lavender requires full sun to grow, with no exceptions. That is the only way to get the best flowers, the best fragrance, and the best oils. The less sun your plants are exposed to, the less it will bloom. Lavender requires a minimum of six hours of sun per day during spring and summer, and if it doesn't get it, its growth will be stunted, and it will likely die.

There is only one way you can revive your lavender if it is planted in the shade. You must dig it up and transfer it to a container - in the right soil - and immediately get it out in the sun.

Lavender needs to see the sun all year round, even in the winter when it is dormant. Make sure your plants are situated in open spaces, not beneath trees or any other form of shade.

If you can get your lavender into the sun in time, you may be able to revive it, but there are no guarantees. Again, you may need to discard the plants and start again, planting them in the right place the next time around.

How to Revive Lavender After Winter

Not all lavender species can survive a harsh winter outdoors in freezing, frosty conditions. The only cold-hardy varieties are hybrids and English lavender – they will tolerate ice, snow, and freezing temperatures. French lavender is more delicate and will not survive.

If you have chosen to grow the Spanish or French lavender, you must grow them in containers so they can be taken indoors in the winter. If your lavender gets damaged by the frost, it will not be easy to revive it, and you will probably have to start again in spring with new plants.

However, remember that, over the winter, lavender goes into a dormant stage. So, it's best to wait until the spring to determine if your plants have survived or not – any signs of green growth, and you know they are okay.

Chapter 5: How to Prune Lavender Plants

Pruning your lavender is an essential part of keeping your plants thriving and healthy and not that hard to do. However, you do need to know what you are doing so you don't over-prune.

Despite there being many varieties of lavender, the overall pruning techniques remain the same. The only real difference is that English lavender, being a hardier variety, can withstand a harder summer pruning than the Spanish or French.

Why You Should Prune Lavender

If this is your first foray into growing lavender, you probably don't realize that pruning is vital to maintaining your plants. Regular pruning helps keep your plants looking nice, encourages them to flower, and stops them from becoming scraggly or too woody.

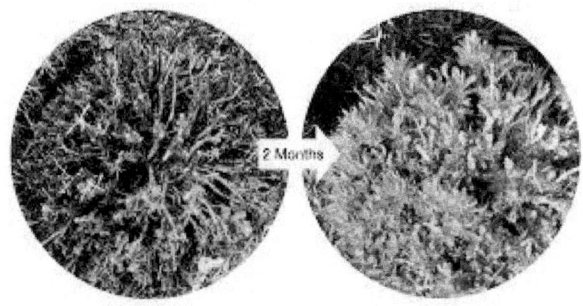

Before you get your pruners and start hacking away at your plants, you need to know how to do it. Taking too much or cutting it wrong can seriously harm the lavender, and you can kill it.

Pruning English Lavender

Otherwise known as Lavandula angustifolia, English lavender is also one of the hardiest. Typically, you get one main flush of blooms from these varieties, but you may get a second one after pruning, although it will be much weaker.

English lavenders can be pruned in early spring to delay flowering – some people do, for their own reasons. However, the main pruning should take place in the summer. Once the plants have flowered, you can do one of two things – leave the flowers to die back or harvest them. After harvesting or the flowers have died, whichever you choose, cut the plants back, leaving up to two inches of foliage on the plant. There must always be some foliage on the stems because the plants cannot regenerate if you cut right down to the wood. Careful pruning can see your lavender plant live for over 20 years.

Pruning Hybrid Lavender

Otherwise called Lavandula x Intermedia, hybrid lavender is a late-season plant, typically blooming from July through August and lasting well into late summer. Like English lavender, these should be pruned once they have flowered, again leaving up to two inches of foliage on the stems. You may have to sacrifice a few late blooms to do this but again, do it right, and your plants can last for years.

Pruning Spanish Lavender

Also called Lavandula stoechas or the Butterfly lavender, these tend to be continuous bloomers, from spring right through to the fall. Because of that, it isn't always easy to work out when the best time to prune is. Generally, you should prune right after the first flush of flowers, again leaving up to two inches of foliage. For the remainder of the season, remove the flowers as they die (called deadheading) and continue to trim them, shaping them into a nice, rounded shape. Spanish lavender typically lives for between five and ten years.

A couple of tips:

- To reiterate, never, ever prune into the woody stems on your lavender. Leafless wood should always be left intact because cutting into it can harm the plant. Always leave some green; otherwise, the plant cannot regenerate – the best rule to follow is to find where the woody part of the stem turns green and flexible. Then, count two leaf nodes above that and prune them just below the third. This will ensure your lavender grows into a stable and healthy plant.

- Always make sure your pruning secateurs or shears are sterilized before use. You can use a solution of hot water and bleach and then wash it off. One of the most common ways diseases are transferred between plants is via dirty equipment, but this can easily be avoided. Also, ensure that they are sharp – you want to make a quick, clean cut that heals easily; you don't want to keep hacking away and causing lots of wounds on the woody stems that may never heal.

When to Prune Lavenders

As a minimum, prune your lavender once per year - if you can do it twice, even better. Pruning stops the lavender from turning into a bundle of wood - when this happens, new growth will not be produced. Additionally, plants that are too woody are more likely to rot or crack during the winter.

- **Spring** - Pruning at this time of the year delays the flowering, and it is also a good time to prune off any damaged or dead parts. Wait until the new growth appears before pruning, and then cut back just enough to leave a few shoots on each branch base.
- **Summer/Fall** - Once the last flush of flowers has faded, your plants can be pruned back hard, leaving an inch of growth on top of the woody stems. This allows for good air circulation and stops snow from collecting on the plant and breaking it. It also prevents strong winds from breaking the weaker branches off.

One thing you must NEVER do is prune your plants just before winter sets in. Lavender requires a cover of foliage to help protect it against the winter, and pruning too late in the year can cause your plants to die from the cold weather.

There are also some guidelines depending on *the age* of your plants:

- **Young Plants** – These must be allowed to establish a good root system. In the first year, new growth should be pruned away to help increase the plant's volume. Young plants should be discouraged from flowering until the second year, so pinch out any flower tips as they appear.
- **Middle-Aged Plants** – Heavy pruning may be required, and you can safely remove up to a third of the branch length, ensuring some new growth is left on each one. This is also the best age to shape your plants, giving them better airflow and spacing the blossoms evenly.
- **Mature Plants** – At this age, you need not hold back, so prune away to your heart's content. Heavy pruning reawakens older stems that have gone dormant, thus making them flower once more.

Pruning Tools

Pruning lavender in the spring requires small pruning shears or snips as these allow you better control, and you can see exactly where the cuts are being made. You can get away with hedging shears or an electric trimmer in the summer if your plants are large enough.

The most important thing is to ensure your tools are clean and sharp.

Pruning Techniques

Wait until you see new growth on the plant before you start trimming it. The reason for this is that you will easily see where the cuts need to be made.

Prune too early, and you will cut off the new growth before it has even started, leading to almost certain death for the plant.

Pruning in the spring is far more precise than in the summer. Summer pruning can be more focused on shaping the lavender plants instead of worrying about where the cuts need to be made.

Again, to repeat - do NOT cut into the woody stems below the foliage. If you cut the plant too far back, it will not recover.

Pruning Lavender in Spring

Before you even think about pruning, look closely at your plants to ensure they have lots of new growth. If they don't, wait a little longer. If there is plenty of growth, it is safe to go ahead.

These are the steps to follow:

Step One

To work out where you need to cut each branch, look for where new leaves are growing. Mostly, you will see these at the bottom of the stems, so, very carefully, move other branches out of the way until you see them. Fresh leaf buds are incredibly fragile, and handling the plant too harshly will just break them off.

If you see a load of scruffy new leaves at the top of a stem, look down the stem to find where the strong, healthy growth is. Cut the plant at the top of that new growth, removing all the ragged bits. This ensures your plant grows fuller and stops it from turning woody.

Step Two

Cut the stems back to a point just above any new growth but be careful that you don't damage or break any new leaves. That said, try to cut as near to those new leaf buds as possible - where dead stems are not cut back, they will be on show all summer - not very attractive.

Step Three

If your plants have any completely dead branches, you can cut these completely to remove them. However, it is strongly recommended that you wait before you do this - lavender is a slow starter, and what you think is dead may not be - they may sprout new growth during the summer. Leave those branches until you do the summer pruning - if there is no growth on them by then, there won't be any. You can prune dead growth all year round as it won't harm the plant.

Pruning Lavender in Summer

Summer pruning is optional, but your plants will reward you if you do it. Typically, this is when you shape your plants to keep them compact and full and to hold off on woody growth appearing.

And if you cut your plants back after flowering, you may even be rewarded with a second flush of flowers.

Once your plant is finished flowering, cut the new growth back by a third or half - no more. Be very careful that none of the branches are cut back below the leaves into the woody growth.

If this is your first time and you are a little nervous, try deadheading the plant instead. All this means is that you remove any dead flower spikes by cutting them down to the main plant.

When you prune your lavender in the summer, keep some of it back to start new plants. Growing lavender from a cutting is simple – choose a cutting with between three and five-leaf nodes on it and plenty of growth at the top.

Remove the three to five bottom sets of leaves and remove any flower heads that have appeared. Pop them in a well-drained soil mix in a pot and leave them somewhere warm and humid – polytunnels or greenhouses are perfect for this. You can also place a plastic bag over the top of the pot to help with the humidity. Keep them moist but never soaking wet, and make sure the soil does not dry out – as soon as you see new growth, usually three to six weeks, you know the plant has rooted.

One of the most important things to remember is to cut your plants back regularly. If you neglect them and never prune them, you will have ugly, woody, scruffy plants.

Tips for Pruning Lavender

Pruning is a critical part of ensuring the health of your plants. If you don't prune lavender, it gets woody and over-sized, forming nooks that trap moisture – this leads to several problems:

- In the summer, trapped moisture can lead to root rot.
- In the late autumn, trapped moisture can bring on early frost, stopping the growing season in its tracks.
- In the water, the moisture will freeze, splitting the woody stems apart. Also, dense or sprawling plants are vulnerable to being loaded with snow, deforming, or breaking the plants.

Regular pruning also prompts stronger root growth, particularly in the winter months when the plant uses its roots for storing energy.

Chapter 6: Harvesting and Storing Lavender

Like most other harvests, lavender gathering must be done at the right time, dependent on several things - the bloom rhythm, temperature, daylight, and rainfall.

If you succeed in growing lavender, harvesting it is the easiest part, and, following on from the previous chapter, the more your lavender is pruned, the better your harvests will be. Both pruning and harvesting encourage the plant to branch, giving it a bushy look.

When to Harvest Lavender

Harvesting lavender should be done early, in more sense than one – early in the spring, early in the blooming time, and early in the morning.

- **Early spring** – When you harvest your flowers early in the spring, the plant has plenty of time to produce more flowers for the summer and fall. This is important where your growing season is short. If you live in a mild, frost-free climate, some lavender varieties will bloom continuously, allowing you to harvest them throughout the year.
- **Early bloom** – When you harvest lavender early in its bloom cycle, you get the highest level of essential oil and the best fragrance. How do you know when to do this? Depending on what you want, when the young flower buds are tight and have hardly bloomed, their oils and fragrance are at their highest, while lavender that has opened fully is more colorful and better for bouquets. The older a lavender flower gets, the more its aroma and oil levels decrease. And once mature, the flowers will drop off the stems, making it harder to dry them. That said, if you don't get round to harvesting early, later is better than not doing it at all – leaving dead flowers requires more energy from the plant and reducing the chances of more vigorous growth.
- **Early morning** – Last, if you are harvesting for the fragrance or the oils, do it first thing in the morning. During that time, the cool night air makes the flowers perky; as the heat rises, some of the essential oils dissipate.

Which Flowers to Harvest

If you are only looking to harvest individual flowers, you must find the right bloom. Then, trace the stem down from the flower to a junction where you can see two new branches, buds, or flower leaves forming.

Use small scissors or snips to cut the stem just above the new side branches or leaves. Once you have removed the flower and center stem, the plant will then send its energy to those new shoots, helping them grow and produce their own flowers.

If you want longer stems or intend to make a bouquet that includes green foliage, follow the stem a bit further down and snip just above another, deeper junction. This might be the best way to harvest compact, smaller lavender plants that don't have so much space between the leaf and bud nodes, or if you want to clip a bit more off a more established plant.

Once you have harvested, you will have a nice bunch of lavender stems.

These bunches are perfect for hanging, drying, or displaying in vases. If you want them as cut flowers in your house, simply place a bunch or a few stems into a vase of water. If you intend to dry them, read on for more instructions.

How to Dry Your Lavender Flowers

Now your lavender is harvested, you can think about drying it, and there are five ways you can do this. Which method you choose is up to you, and I will give you the pros and cons of each method to help you make your mind up.

Hanging Lavender

The easiest way of drying your lavender is to hang it:

1. Collect bundles of a hand-bouquet size and use a rubber band or twine to secure the stems. Hang them upside down somewhere dry and warm and leave them to dry.

2. If your harvest is large, split it into several bundles - too much lavender in a bundle will take a longer time to dry and could end up rotting. Smaller bundles allow for more airflow and quicker drying.

3. For the same reason, the stems should not be tied too tightly – just enough that they do not fall apart but not so tight that it damages the stems.

4. Lavender should be hung in a warm, dry location where there is decent airflow. This can be outside if your weather permits or indoors near an open window. You can also use a fan to help the air circulate. If you want, dry your lavender in the dark; it will retain its color much better.

5. It can take anywhere from a week or two to more than a month for the lavender to dry. To see how dry it is, try breaking a stem – if it bends, it isn't dry. Fully dried lavender stems snap in half easily.

6. If you want, you can stand the bunches upright, perhaps in an empty vase, to dry; however, upright lavender may flop and not dry straight.

This method works best in climates that are naturally dry and arid or indoors in controlled conditions.

Using a Food Dehydrator

Yes, you can use a food dehydrator to dry your lavender! It is an easy process, much quicker than leaving the lavender to hang dry. This method works best if you are using lavender to make salves or infused oil. It speeds up the process and ensures your lavender is completely dry. If your lavender is not 100% dry, the remaining moisture can cause your oils to develop mold, which will spoil it completely.

The important thing to remember is not to overheat the lavender. Otherwise, you can lose many of the therapeutic benefits and some of the essential oils. Your food dehydrator should be set to the lowest temperature, no higher than 100 to 105°F.

Here's how to do this:

1. Harvest your fresh lavender. Although you will only dry the flower buds, you should still harvest with the stems as it keeps them looking fresh.

2. Gather your lavender with the buds evenly lined up and trim off the stems – you can throw these in your compost heap.

3. Lay the buds out in a single layer in the dehydrator. Use liners if your flowers are crumbly or your trays have large gaps in them. Alternatively, use parchment paper.

4. Set the dehydrator to a low setting and leave it - it will take between 24 and 48 hours to fully dry, depending on the variety, bud size, and the machine you are using. To see if they are dry, try to break one of the largest buds - if it is dry and crumbly and the center stem snaps, it is done.

5. Transfer your dried buds to an airtight container until you are ready to use them.

In Baskets or on Screens

The third way is to use screens or large baskets to dry your lavender. All you do is ay them flat, drying the buds or the entire flower with the stem.

You can also build your own drying racks, consisting of one or more framed, flat screens. However you do it, flat-drying lavender still requires it to be arid and warm, and it still needs time. The lavender flowers should be spread in one layer so plenty of air can flow between them.

In the Oven

Using your oven to dry lavender is easy and quick:

1. Preheat the oven to about 200°F (or 100°C).

2. Line a baking tray with aluminum foil and lay the lavender in a thin layer on the sheet.

3. Put it in the preheated oven and leave for around 10 minutes or until the stalks are brittle. Do NOT close the oven door - leave it open slightly, allowing moisture to pass through. If the stalks still feel moist, rotate them and dry them for a further five minutes.

4. Remove the dry lavender and use your hand to push the flowers gently off the stalks into a container - be careful as the flowers may be a little prickly.

In the Microwave

This is much like drying it in the oven, but first, you need to remove the flowers from the leaves and stems. Layer the lavender thinly over two layers of paper towel and put it in the microwave.

Run the microwave on high for around a minute, and then check if it is dry. If not, continue for 20 seconds at a time until the lavender is dry through.

With both the oven and microwave drying techniques, you must monitor it properly, or the flowers can burn, and the paper towel may catch fire.

Storing Dried Lavender

After your lavender has dried, it must be properly stored until you are ready to use it. This ensures the fragrance is preserved, the color stays bright, and the taste and efficacy are also preserved.

There are lots of ways you can store your lavender to ensure decent shelf life, and these tips will help ensure your harvest remains safe and usable:

- **An airtight container** – Mason jars are ideal as they keep the lavender away from the air. Dried lavender exposed to the air for any length of time will turn stale.

- **In a dark place** – When dried lavender is exposed to the sun, it can lose its color and start to decay. It should be stored somewhere dark and cool, like a drawer or cupboard. You can also use colored glass jars to keep the sun out.

- **Low humidity and a stable temperature** – If your lavender is stored where the temperature and humidity levels fluctuate, mold can form, ruining the lavender.

- **Only when 100% dry** – Never store lavender that hasn't dried completely because even the slightest bit of moisture can cause mold to form.

- **With the blooms and stalks separated** - The flowers should be removed from the stalk before storing lavender. Do this by rubbing a stalk gently between your hands or running your hand down the stem. The stalks can be discarded.

Using these easy tips, you can harvest, dry, and store your lavender using the methods that work best for you. Don't be afraid to experiment with the drying methods - one will always work better than the rest, depending on your climate.

Lastly, do not use cheap containers to store the dried lavender in. Paying for the best quality will ensure longer shelf life and a better product.

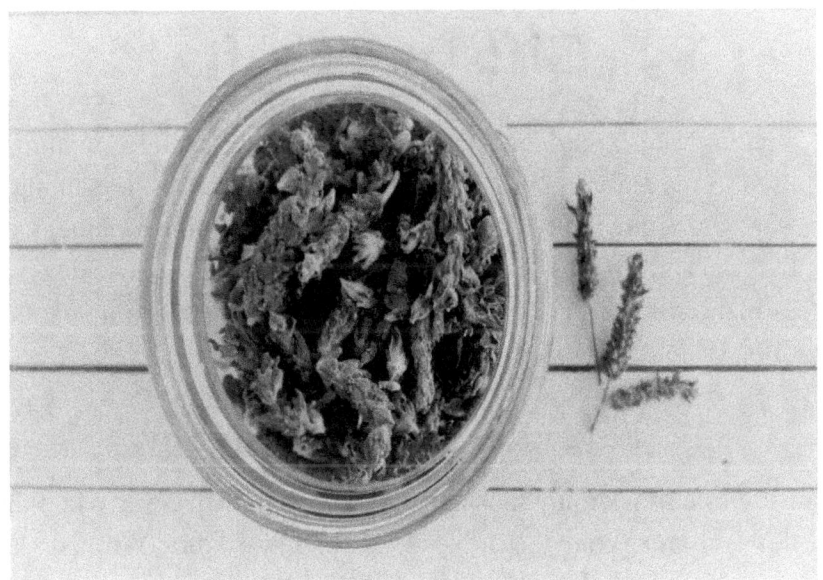

Chapter 7: Simple Lavender Gifts and Crafts

Crafting with lavender is one of the ancient arts, and everything is used in the crafting - the flowers, leaves, and stems – depending on what you are making. Popular crafts revolve around cooking, scent, baskets, and wreaths so, here are some of the easiest lavender crafts to make. In a later chapter, we'll look at the more complex crafts using lavender oil, but these are simple to follow.

Lavender Sachets – No-Sew

I use lace trim on my sachets, but you can use whatever you want – this is a great craft to use up some of those fabric remnants and scraps you might have lying around.

What You Need:
- Lace trim or other trim fabric – at least two inches wide
- A hot glue gun and glue sticks
- Dried lavender buds
- Ribbons
- Sharp scissors

What to Do

Step One

Cut a length of trimming fabric- it should be 28 inches long by at least two inches wide.

Step Two

Using the glue gun, place a thin line of glue on the inside edge of the fabric. It should be enough that it will seal but not so much you can see glue coming through the fabric. The same needs to be done along both edges of your fabric.

Step Three

Fold the glued fabric in half, making a thickness of four layers, seven inches long. You are trying to create a small pouch of two layers on each side, which will hold your lavender buds. Glue the edges together but leave the last two inches on each side unglued.

Step Four

Spoon your lavender buds into the bag, filling it about two-thirds of the way.

Step Five

Pinch the bag together at the top and use a piece of ribbon to tie it tightly.

This is what it should look like - depending on the baric you used, of course.

Lavender Ball

Lavender balls are simple to make and make wonderful gifts or ornaments in your own home.

What You Need:

- Styrofoam balls, enough for the number of balls you want to make
  - A paper plate
  - Ribbon
  - White glue
  - Dried lavender
  - Wood skewers - optional
  - A vase - optional

What to Do:

Step One

Pour glue onto the paper plate

Step Two

Roll the balls with the glue, being careful not to get it on your hands

Step Three

Roll the glued balls in the lavender, covering the whole ball - there should be no Styrofoam left exposed.

Step Four

Leave them to dry off overnight and then form a small piece of ribbon into a bow and use a dot of glue to attach it to the ball. Once dry, you can place them in bowls or glasses around your house.

You can also pop each ball onto a skewer and place several into the vase.

This craft has so many variants that you can experiment with it for hours. Try using different ball sizes, different vases, or bowls to display them, or even use a mixture of dried herbs with the lavender to create your own unique scents.

Lavender Wands

Lavender wands, woven properly, will retain their scent for some time and, when the wand begins to lose the scent, you have only to squeeze it, and it will release more.

Lavender is one of the top choices for aromatherapy simply because it has such relaxing qualities. Combine a lavender wand with some lavender bath bombs or bath salts, and you have the ingredients for a super-relaxing pamper kit. And, because lavender is reported to help you sleep, placing a wand under your pillow can ensure a good night's sleep. They even make good air fresheners for the car – so long as they don't make you sleepy!

What You Need:

- Lavender flowers with long stems. Somewhere between 7 in and 15 in, so long as it is an odd number
- Two yards of ribbon (1/4 inch)
- Sharp scissors
- A toothpick
- A spoon

What to Do:

Step One

Lay your lavender stems beside each other, arranging the flowers in two rows.

This will ensure your wand is long and slim. If you lay them all at the same level, you would have a short and fat wand.

Step Two

Tie a piece of ribbon at the base of the flower heads, around the stems. Leave a loose end of at least 10 inches – this will be used to make a knot later on. The other end of the ribbon should remain attached to the spool – in my case, an elastic band.

Step Three

Using the edge of the spoon, squash the stems gently. This will ensure you can bend them without snapping them.

Step Four

Bend the lavender stems back to make a cage surrounding the flower. The loose ribbon end should be run beside the flowers, coming out at the bottom of your cage, while the other end, attached to your spool, should come out at the top of the cage.

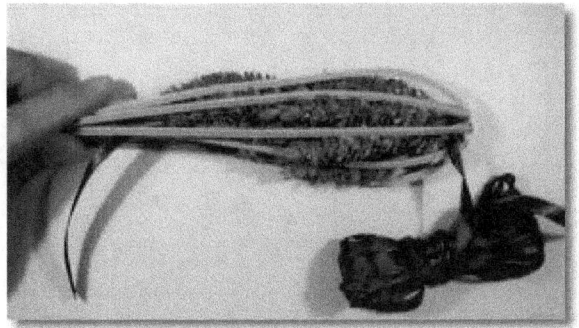

Step Five

Take the end of the ribbon attached to the spool and weave it over and under the stems.

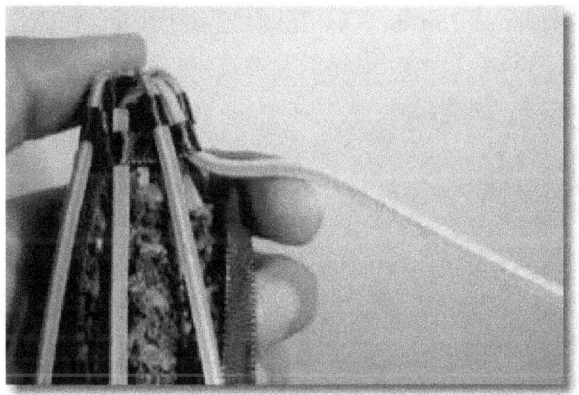

Step Six

If any bits of flower poke out of the cage between the ribbon and stems, use the toothpick to pop them back in.

Step Seven

Continue weaving the ribbon until you get to the end of the flowers. Go back to the beginning, pulling the ribbon as tight as you can. Any slack ribbon should be worked through, tightening the weaving into a snug bundle. As the lavender dries, it shrinks, which is why tight weaving is important.

Step Eight

Take the end of the ribbon at the spool and wrap it a few times around the base, tying it with the loose end that comes out of the bottom of the cage.

That's it; your finished lavender wand!

Lavender Hearts

Lavender hearts make great gifts for your nan or your mum, and you can even treat yourself to one too. They look great hanging in your house, and they smell wonderful.

What You Need

- Two types of fabric, whatever pattern or colors you want
- Some ribbon
- Needle
- Embroidery floss
- Scissors
- About ¼ cup of dried lavender
- A small funnel - or you can use a rolled piece of paper
- A pencil
- A heart template - there are plenty on the internet, something like this

What to Do

Step One

Print your heart template and cut it out around the outer shape. Trace this twice onto one piece of your fabric and cut them out - the size you cut out is up to you.

Step Two

Next, trim the template to meet the inner heart and trace around this on the other piece of fabric - just once, this time - and cut it out.

Step Three

Now pin the small heart onto one of the bigger ones in the center and hand-stitch it on. Or, if you have a sewing machine handy, use that.

Step Four

Pin this to the second larger heart.

Step Five

Use a simple stitch to sew the two pieces together and stop about an inch from where your stitches started. Hide the knotted end inside the heart so it cannot be seen.

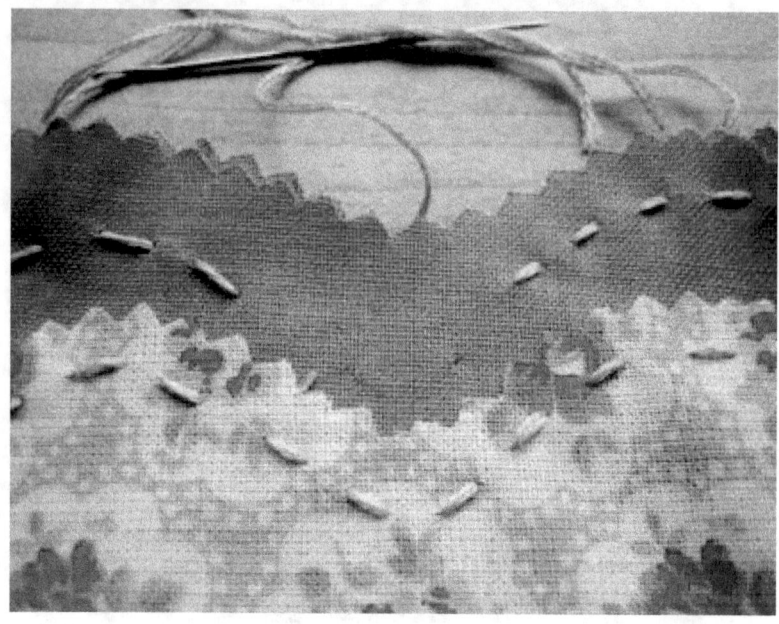

Step Six

Use a funnel or a piece of paper to fill the heart with your lavender.

Step Seven

Finish sewing the heart together, adding a ribbon loop.

Reusable Lavender Dryer Bags

Lavender can be used to make these neat reusable lavender dryer bags, leaving your clothes smelling amazing.

What You Need:

- Drawstring organza bags - available in most dollar stores
- Dried lavender

What to Do

These really couldn't be easier! Spoon dried lavender into the bags and pull the drawstring closed, tying it to keep it tight.

That really is all there is to it! If you are feeling extra handy, you can get some material and make your own bags, so long as they are sewn tightly enough and have a drawstring or Velcro strip to keep them closed while in the dryer - you don't want the lavender spilling out all over the place.

Lavender Wreath

Lavender wreaths can be dead simple or as intricate as you want, and you can use any flowers you want. Lavender is the best, though, and can make a wonderful, simple wreath.

What You Need

- Flowering stems. You will need a lot of these, so you can either harvest your own when it flowers or buy bunches from a lavender farm.
- A circular base – you can purchase grapevine or willow bases at reasonable prices at any craft store, or you may find them in garden centers, or you can use a wooden ring.
- Elastic bands
- Scissors or snips
- A ball of twine, wire, or raffia

What to Do

Step One

Arrange a handful of lavender, so the flowers are bunched tightly together. Then cut the stems a few inches under the blossoms and hold them together with an elastic band.

Step Two

Lay the lavender bunch on your base and secure it using wire, twine, or whatever you have on hand.

Step Three

Repeat with another bunch, ensuring it overlaps the first bunch's stems and bind it to the base.

Step Four

Continue all the way around the base, making sure the flowers all point the same way and, when you get to the last one, tuck the twine or wire beneath the first bunch of lavender.

Step Five

Make a hanging loop, attach it to the base, and leave the wreath flat so it dries and the flowers don't droop.

You can embellish your wreath however you want or just hang it as it is. It will last for years, but should the scent fade; you can always add a couple of drops of lavender essential oil to the back.

Lavender and Lime Potpourri

Who can resist the fresh, relaxing scent of lavender combined with the refreshing scent of lime? Making potpourri is quite easy, and it takes little time either. Ingredients can be found in your garden and grocery store, and lavender is one of the best ingredients you can use.

Feel free to tweak this recipe as you want to suit you:

What You Need

- A whole fresh lime
- A few handfuls of dried lavender
- A couple of handfuls of mini pinecones, alder cones, or cedar roses
- A handful of other dried flowers, such as hydrangea, to decorate it
- Lime fragrance oil
- Ground ginger – optional

What to Do

Step One

Peel and slice the limes and place them in the oven overnight at 30°C. Alternatively, you can place them in your airing cupboard and leave them to dry out for a few days.

Step Two

Put the cones or cedar roses into a Tupperware container or plastic bag and add a couple of drops of the lime oil. Shake well to coat and leave them for a few hours to let the oil soak into them.

Step Three

Mix the lavender, limes, cones, and ginger powder (if using) in a bowl and scatter the dried flower petals over the top.

Warning - Do not allow this to come into contact with any textiles, or painted, polished, or synthetic surfaces.

This makes sufficient potpourri for a bowl, and it will go perfectly in a kitchen or a bathroom. It probably isn't a good idea to use it in your bedroom as the refreshing lime will overpower the relaxing lavender!

Alternatively, you can place it in a pretty drawstring bag and give it as a gift.

Wedding Confetti Cones

You can use paper cones for all sorts of things, such as sweets and potpourri, but these are also a great way of holding wedding confetti. You can buy paper cones, but they are not cheap, whereas one sheet of heavy A4 paper will make two cones.

You Will Need:

- A4 paper
- Dried lavender

What to Do:

Step One

Using a ruler as your hard edge, tear your paper into squares of 15 cm. Each A4 sheet will make two squares with a little bit left over.

Step Two

Make each square into a cone, using one corner folded into a point and rolling the paper into a cone shape. Stick the overlap down into the cone

Step Three

When it has dried, pour dried lavender into the cones.

These make wonderful confetti cones, using biodegradable materials as the confetti.

Tips

Instead of cutting the paper, tear it – it looks more professional.

How big your overlap is will determine how much lavender it can hold – if you don't want much, have a bigger overlap.

If you can get high-tack glue, use that to stick the overlap down. This ensures the cones won't fall apart while they are drying.

You can use any paper you like – it need not be plain – so long as it is heavyweight enough not to crumple.

Lavender Christmas Ball Ornaments

Lavender Christmas ornaments are simple to make and last forever.

What You Need:

- Clear glass or plastic Christmas ornament balls - buy them or use existing ornament balls
- Dried lavender
- A small funnel

What to Do:

Step One

Remove the tops from the ball ornaments - they should come off easily enough but, if you are using glass balls, be careful as the glass is quite thin.

Step Two

Using a small funnel, pour dried lavender into the balls and put the tops back on. Tie a thin piece of ribbon on it to hang it on your tree

Lavender Eye Pillow

Everyone has seen eye masks or eye pillows in the stores, and some of us have even used them before. Some have elastic to hold them on your face, while others are just laid over the top of your eyes for relaxation and de-stressing. Making your own eye pillow is simple to do, and you can have it in any fabric color or design you want. You can even have a zipper or Velcro on one side to make refilling easier – the only limit here is your imagination.

What You Need:

- Floral or plain fabric – your choice. Use two colors for a contrast
- Dried lavender flowers
- ½ cup of rice – optional

What to Do:

Step One

Measure your fabric into rectangles of about eight to nine inches in length and three inches in width – make sure you have a seam allowance of half an inch on each side. If you want a full pillow, make it a bit bigger.

Step Two

Place the rectangles together, inside out, and stitch on three sides using a sewing machine or sew it by hand.

Step Three

Turn the rectangle the right way out and fill it with your lavender or a mixture of rice and lavender. If you want a zipper or Velcro in it, you will need to add it now or just sew the rectangle shut.

When you are not using your eye pillow, keep it in a Ziploc bag to retain the fragrance. You can also pop it in the freezer for a while, so you have a nice, cool, refreshing eye pillow for hot days.

Lavender Fire Bundles

When you are done harvesting your lavender, don't discard the stems. And if you have old bundles of lavender, don't throw those away either – I will show you how to turn them into fire bundles. Throwing these on a fire will help them release the remaining scent left in the flowers. They make a wonderful fire starter, and they date back many years. And, if you have a firepit outdoors, throw a couple on it – it will help keep the insects away from you!

What You Need:

- Lavender stems or old bundles of lavender
- Twine or raffia
- Fabric scraps for wrapping around the bundles – optional

What to Do:

Step One

Make your stems into small bundles and wrap a piece of fabric around the center. If you make a three-inch bundle, use a piece of fabric about seven inches by two inches. If you are using old dried lavender bundles, just tie a piece of fabric or twine around them.

Step Two

Place them in a pile or a basket beside your fire!

That is all you have to do. The fabric is a nice touch to make them look nice, especially if you give them a gift. Do make sure your raffia or fabric is natural and not synthetic. If you are only using them for yourself and you don't need them to look pretty, just use a piece of natural twine or a green stem to tie around them.

Chapter 8: Cooking with Lavender

Lavender is best known for its heady fragrance and, while most people use it in cut flower arrangements or crafts, few people realize that it can also be used in cooking, too - for both savory and sweet dishes.

Some who use lavender in their food complain that it tastes soapy, but it really shouldn't taste like that. Lavender can bring the best out in any dish if used properly in the right quantities

Lavender complements peppery and herby dishes, brings out the richness in fruits, adds depth and just a little intrigue to roasted vegetables and meat, and enhances sweet foods with honeyed, floral highlights.

What Makes Lavender "Culinary?"

Not all lavender is meant to be eaten, and the term "culinary" refers to two things - the type (cultivar) and how the lavender is processed. For cooking, some cultivars perform far better than others. The most popular cultivars are all from the English lavender species:

- Lavandula Angustifolia - Folgate

- Lavandula Angustifolia – Melissa
- Lavandula Angustifolia - Croxton's Wild
- Lavandula Angustifolia – Wykoff
- Lavandula Angustifolia – Miss Katherine
- Lavandula Angustifolia – Royal Velvet
- Lavandula Angustifolia - Buena Vista

Any one of these cultivars, known as True Lavender, is suitable for culinary use. However, know they all have their own distinct taste, and what you grow for cooking with will depend on the taste you want. For example, the Melissa cultivar is a little peppery, while Miss Katherine has a definite floral, sweet taste, and Croxton's Wild is more earthy and a hint of cinnamon. Two of the best cultivars are Folgate and Buena Vista, both good all-rounders.

Lavandins, on the other hand, are the hybrids - x Intermedia - and their flavor is resinous, pungent, and can give your dishes a bitter taste.

The Process

To use your lavender for cooking, you need to harvest it at the right time, when between 25 and 50% of the buds on each stem are in flower. If the buds still have a green hue, they are not ready for harvest.

Next, your lavender needs to be dried in bundles, as described in an earlier chapter. Then you can gently remove the dried buds and flowers from the stems before cleaning them - sifting through your dried flowers to remove any bits of stem or leaves.

Lavender for culinary use must be sifted often, ensuring that you have only dried flowers or buds, nothing else. Ensure that the protective layer around the flower is also removed. This is called the calyx:

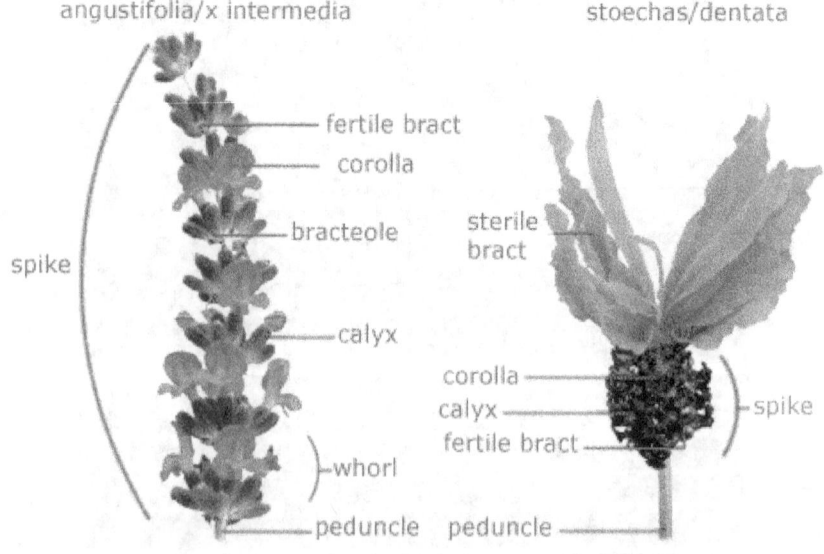

Which Part to Eat?

Only the flower bud is suitable for eating. If you are making lavender tea, you can get away with the odd bit of stem or leaf, but these taste more bitter than the flowers and affect your dish's overall taste. They are tough and not pleasant to bite into.

Back to the question of lavender foods tasting of soap – there are two reasons for this. The first is that you used the wrong lavender cultivar, and the second is that you used too much.

Lavender doesn't just have a strong aroma. It also has a strong taste, particularly when you grow high-quality organic lavender and process and store it correctly. "Less is more" really is true for using lavender in cooking, and a little bit goes an awful long way. The perfect amount is when you can only just detect it, and that is when it enhances the other flavors in the dish.

Using lavender in cooking became popular across the Mediterranean and was soon being used in Italian, French, Spanish, and English dishes in the 17th century. From then on, the most popular choice has been the English lavender, given it has a mild taste, almost a floral, peppery flavor.

What Lavender Tastes Like

When you first taste lavender, it tastes and smells strongly of flowers but with hints of earthy, herbaceous, minty flavors. Some lavender varieties can also have a fruity, woody, or smoky flavor, making it one of the most complex culinary herbs.

How to Use Lavender in Cooking

Lavender is unique in flavor and aroma and can be used fresh or dried in your cooking. However, when you use dried lavender, be aware that the flavor is more intense, and, as such, you should be sparing in your use of it. The best way to use it is to add it a little at a time until you get the flavor just right – if you use too much, your food will taste bitter and as though you are eating heavily perfumed food.

The lavender flavor goes well with other herbs, such as rosemary, thyme, sage, and oregano. Often, French lavender is used as an ingredient in Herbes de Provence, which I will explain how to make later in this chapter. Typically, you can use fresh lavender as you would fresh rosemary in a dish, such as bread and meat marinades.

Lavender flowers can be used as a garnish on desserts or salads, and fresh lavender flowers can be added to a tossed salad to bring a little color. The buds can be added to ice cream, in wine, or even on top of a cake.

You can find lavender at farmers' markets, both dried and fresh, if you don't want to grow your own or can't wait for it to grow. It is an incredible ingredient to keep in your kitchen, but do be careful that your food doesn't end up tasting and smelling like a potpourri!

Remember the following tips when you experiment with using lavender in your cooking:

1. Regardless of what dish you are using lavender in, make sure it is culinary lavender. In the same way that coconut oil is, lavender is produced for specific uses. While culinary lavender is perfectly okay to eat, ornamental grade lavender is not. While it won't do you any harm, it won't taste so nice.

2. Lavender should be used as an infusion in your cooking. Rather than chucking whole lavender stems, complete with flowers and leaves in, grind the lavender first for baking or add it to liquids, and then strain it out, so you only get a hint of the flavor.

3. Don't use too much. Unless you are following a trusted recipe, one you have tried often before, be sparing in how much you use. It is strong, and its flavor can detract

from other flavors in your food. Too little is better than too much,

4. Because of its strong flavor, lavender should be paired with other strong flavors. If you are baking, use very little or balance it out with lemon zest and juice. Herbes de Provence, for example, goes perfectly with chicken and lamb dishes.

Now let's get on to some recipes!

Lavender Shortbread

Ingredients:

For the Glaze:

- Whites from three large eggs
- 4 cups of powdered/icing sugar
- ½ tsp cream of tartar

For the Shortbread:

- 1/3 cup rice flour
- 2 ½ cups all-purpose flour
- 1 ½ tsp kosher salt
- 1 cup room-temperature unsalted butter plus six extra tbsp, cut into pieces
- 1 tsp coarse-ground dried lavender
- ¾ cup granulated sugar

You will also need two fluted cutters, one 3-1/8 inch, and one 1-¼ inch diameter.

Instructions

To make the glaze:

1. Stir the egg whites, cream of tartar, and powdered sugar together in a bowl. Use a rubber spatula or wooden spoon and stir until the mixture resembles a thick paste. It must have no dry spots in it.

While you can use it immediately once your cookies have cooled off, it is best if left for at least 12 hours to allow the sugar time to hydrate fully. You can also make it a week in advance and leave it in the refrigerator in a covered container – it should be brought to room temperature before you use it.

To make the shortbread:

0. Whisk the salt, all-purpose flour, and rice flour in a bowl.

1. With an electric mixer set on medium-high, beat the sugar, butter, and lavender for about five minutes, or until pale and fluffy.

2. Add the dry ingredients and set the mixer to low, mixing until fully incorporated.

3. Wrap the mixture in plastic wrap and leave to chill for between two hours and two days.

4. Preheat the oven to 350°F.

5. Lightly flour two sheets of parchment dough and roll the dough between them to 1/8 inch thick.

6. Use the large cutter to cut 16 cookie rounds and reroll the scraps.

7. With the small cutter, punch centers out of the rounds.

8. Line a baking sheet with parchment paper and bake the cookies for about 12 to 14 minutes or until the edges turn golden.

9. Leave to cool on a wire rack and then quickly dip the cookies into the glaze.

10. Allow the excess to drip off and place on a wire rack. Sprinkle a little extra dried lavender over the top to decorate.

This shortbread can be stored for up to one week in an airtight container at room temperature.

Lavender Sugar

Lavender sugar is perfect for baking and is easy to use. Consider keeping a jar of lavender sugar in your pantry at all times. You can add it to drinks or baked goods, and it requires just two simple ingredients. It only takes a few minutes, and you get a scented sugar that tastes lightly of lavender.

Do NOT use lavender sugar in recipes where a sugar syrup needs to be boiled. The bits of lavender could make the sugar crystallize, and the recipe simply won't work.

Scale this recipe as per your needs.

Ingredients:

- 2 cups sugar
- 1 tbsp dried culinary lavender

Instructions:

0. Put the lavender into your food processor or a food chopper and chop it until it is in small pieces – about 10 to 15 seconds should be enough.

1. Add a cup of sugar and continue blending for a further 15 to 20 seconds. The lavender will be ground finely and mixed with the sugar.

2. Pour it into a bowl, add the remaining sugar, and whisk together.

3. Decant into an airtight container and use as needed.

Stored at room temperature in an airtight container, lavender sugar will keep for six months.

Lavender-Infused Honey

Ingredients:

- 340 g (a cup) honey
- 2 tbsp dried lavender

Instructions:

0. Put the honey in a heavy pan over medium heat. Make sure the pan is large enough as the honey can boil over.

1. Add the lavender and allow the honey to come to a boil.

2. Leave it to boil for five minutes, allowing the lavender to infuse, and then remove the pan from the heat.

3. Pour the honey through a fine sieve into a container - it must be heat-proof.

4. Leave it to cool down to room temperature - it will take about an hour.

5. Store in an airtight container until you are ready to use it.

Lavender Honey Ice Cream

Ingredients:

- 2 cups whole milk
- 1/3 cup honey
- ¼ cup dried culinary lavender
- 5 egg yolks
- ¼ cup sugar
- 1 cup heavy cream

Instructions:

0. Combine the lavender, milk, and honey in a medium pan and bring the mixture to a gentle boil.
1. Cover and remove the pan from the heat, leaving it to steep for about five minutes.
2. Strain it, discarding the lavender and retaining the milk.
3. Use an electric mixer to beat the sugar and egg yolks together to a thick, pale yellow color – about three to five minutes on a medium-high speed.

4. Bring the milk to a simmer over medium-low heat and add half of it to the egg mixture.

5. Whisk to blend it and then stir it into the rest of the milk.

6. Cook on low heat, constantly stirring, until the mixture thickens enough to coat a wooden spoon.

7. Remove the pan from the heat and stir the cream in straight away.

8. Strain the mixture into a bowl and immediately place it in ice water – leave it until the mixture is chilled, stirring it occasionally.

9. Transfer the mixture to an ice cream maker and freeze as per the manufacturer's guide.

The ice cream will store for up to two weeks in an airtight plastic container.

Roast Chicken Glazed with Lavender Honey

Ingredients:

- A whole chicken, approximately 5 to 6 lbs., quartered
- 2 tsp dried culinary lavender
- 1 tbsp dried thyme
- 1 tbsp dried rosemary
- Salt and black pepper to taste
- ½ tsp crushed red pepper flakes
- ¼ cup balsamic vinegar
- ½ cup organic, pure honey

Instructions:

0. Preheat the oven to 400°F and place an oven rack in the center.
1. Season the chicken with salt and pepper to taste and place it in a single layer on a baking tray.
2. Bake for about 20 minutes.
3. Meanwhile, put the lavender, rosemary, thyme, honey, vinegar, and red pepper flakes into a pan over medium-low heat.
4. Whisk the mixture until blended and when, warmed through, remove it from the heat and leave to cool.
5. Baste the cooking chicken with the honey glaze every five minutes until the chicken is thoroughly cooked – a meat thermometer should read 165°F when inserted into the thickest part. This should take 15 to 20 minutes.
6. Take the chicken out of the oven and cover it with foil. Leave to rest for about five minutes before serving.

Lavender Sorbet

Ingredients:

- 1 cup granulated sugar
- 2 cups water
- 2 ½ tbsp freshly squeezed lemon juice
- 1 tbsp dried culinary lavender
- 2 tbsp vodka

Instructions

0. Combine the water and sugar in a pan over medium heat, stirring until the sugar has dissolved.

1. Add the lavender and stir until the mixture begins boiling. Turn the heat to low and simmer for about five minutes.

2. Remove the pan from the heat, cover it and leave it to stand for about ten minutes.

3. Pour the mixture through a fine-mesh strainer into a bowl and discard the flowers.

4. Add the vodka and lemon juice to the mixture and stir until combined. Vodka is the real key to a nice, soft sorbet because alcohol doesn't freeze – adding just a splash to a sorbet will stop it from freezing into a hard ball, and vodka won't affect the taste in any way.

5. Place the mixture into an ice cream maker and process as per the instructions on your machine.

6. If you don't have an ice cream maker, pour the mixture into a container, and cover it. Place in the freezer and, when it has semi solidified, mash it with a fork and freeze it again. When frozen, put it in a blender and blend it into a smooth mixture. Cover it and freeze it again until you need it.

Berry Salad with a Lemon Lavender Vinaigrette

Ingredients

For the Vinaigrette:

- ¼ cup extra virgin olive oil
- 1 minced clove of garlic
- 2 tbsp lemon juice
- 1 tsp honey
- ¼ tsp salt
- ¼ tsp dried culinary lavender buds

For the Salad:

- 3 good handfuls of greens
- ½ cup almonds
- 1 cup mixed berries
- ¼ cup goat cheese, crumbled
- ½ a ripe avocado, sliced

Instructions:

    0. Whisk the vinaigrette ingredients together until fully blended.
    1. Toss the greens with the almonds, cheese, and berries.
    2. Add the vinaigrette and gently toss the salad.
    3. Add the sliced avocado and serve.

Tips

Your lavender buds can be ground using a mortar and pestle or a coffee grinder.

If you cannot buy crumbled cheese, put some soft goat cheese into the freezer for five minutes or so, and then it will crumble.

Lavender and Pepita Brittle

Ingredients:

- ½ cup pepitas – green pumpkin seeds, hulled
- 1 tbsp dried culinary lavender
- ¼ tsp salt

For the Brittle:

- Vegetable cooking spray
- 1 ½ cups granulated sugar
- ½ cup light corn syrup

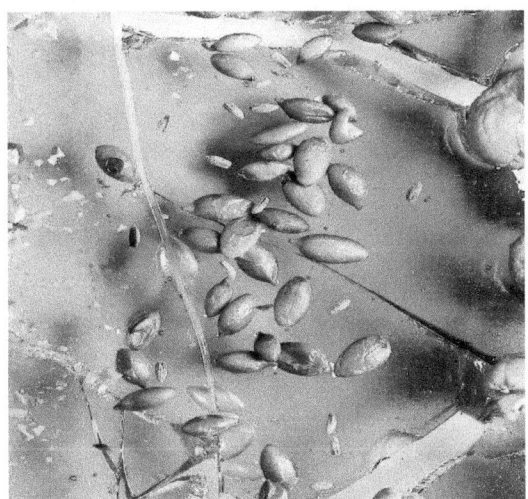

Instructions:

0. Coat a baking sheet, approximately 12 inches by 17 inches, with vegetable cooking spray.

1. In a medium saucepan, bring the corn syrup and sugar to a boil, stirring constantly and using a wet pastry brush to brush the sides of the pan – this stops the sugar from crystallizing on the sides. Keep doing this until the sugar has dissolved.

2. Continue to cook, occasionally swirling it around until it starts to turn a golden color around the edges.

3. Add the pepitas, lavender, and salt and stir to distribute evenly.

4. Continue cooking, occasionally stirring until the mixture turns a pale amber color – around eight minutes.

5. Pour it onto the prepared baking tray – do not spread it out. Leave to cool and then break it into reasonably sized bits.

Lavender Lemonade

Ingredients:

- 6 cups water
- ½ cup sugar
- 3 tbsp dried culinary lavender
- ¼ cup honey
- 2 cups lemon juice
- Lavender petals and lemon slices for garnishing
- OPTIONAL – blue or purple food coloring

Instructions:

0. Mix two cups of water with the sugar and heat over medium heat. Bring to a boil, stirring, until all the sugar has dissolved.

1. Turn the heat off and stir the lavender and honey in.

2. Leave the mixture to steep. It should be around two hours or less, depending on how much of a lavender flavor you want.

3. Strain the mixture, pressing down on the lavender in the strainer to get as much of the juice as you can into the mixture.

4. Pour the lavender liquid into a pitcher, add the lemon juice and the rest of the water, and stir well.

5. If you want a lavender color, add a couple of drops of purple or blue food coloring – not too much, though.

6. Garnish with lemon slices and lavender and serve over ice.

Lavender Spritzer

Ingredients:

- 4 cups water
- ½ cup sugar
- 3 tbsp dried culinary lavender
- 4 ½ cups chilled sparkling water

Instructions:

0. Bring the sugar and plain water to a boil in a large pan, constantly stirring until all the sugar has dissolved.

1. Add the lavender and remove the mixture from the heat.

2. Leave it for 30 minutes (less time if you don't want a strong lavender taste) and then strain it.

3. Return the mixture to the pan and boil it again, reducing it by 50% - about five minutes.

4. Leave to cool off.

5. Pour ¾ cup of sparkling water into each glass and add a ¼ cup of the lavender syrup.

6. Stir well, garnish, and serve.

Lavender and Apricot Rice Pilaf

Ingredients:

- 3 tbsp butter
- ½ cup chopped onion
- 1 cup celery, sliced thinly
- 1 clove peeled garlic, mashed
- 1 cup rice
- 2 ½ cups chicken broth
- 1 tbsp candied ginger
- 2 tbsp dried lavender buds (4 tbsp if using fresh)
- 1 tsp salt
- ¼ cup currants
- ½ cup dried apricots, chopped
- 2 tbsp lemon juice
- ½ cup toasted almonds or chopped pistachios
- 2 tbsp chopped parsley, fresh
- 2 ½ tbsp chopped spearmint, fresh

Instructions:

0. Melt the butter in a medium pan, and then add the celery and onion. Cook until the vegetables have wilted
1. Add the rice and garlic and stir until coated in the butter
2. Add the salt, ginger, broth, and lavender and bring to a boil
3. Turn the heat down to low, cover, and cook until all the liquid is absorbed – do not stir
4. Stir the apricots, lemon juice, and currants into the tender rice and remove from the heat
5. Leave to stand, allowing the fruit to soften, and then add the herbs and nuts, stirring well to mix
6. Serve straight away

Lavender Caramel Sauce

Ingredients:

- 2 cups heavy cream
- 1 tbsp dried culinary lavender
- ¼ cup honey
- ¾ cup light corn syrup or golden syrup
- 2 cups sugar
- 3 tbsp unsalted butter, chopped into chunks
- ¼ tsp fine sea salt

You will also need a wooden spoon or silicone spatula and a candy thermometer.

Instructions:

Start making your sauce 24 hours before you need it:

    1. Combine the cream and lavender and refrigerate in a covered bowl between eight and twelve hours.

2. Strain the cream, pressing the lavender to get as much liquid as you can from it.

3. Heat the cream until you see small bubbles forming at the edge of the pan.

4. Remove it from the heat, cover it and leave it to one side.

5. In a heavy pan, mix the honey, sugar, syrup, and salt and cook on medium heat. Stir it, cooking until you see the mixture starting to simmer at the edges.

6. Use a wet pastry brush to wash the syrup from the sides of the pan and then cover it and cook for three minutes.

7. Take the cover off and brush the sides down again and then attach your thermometer - do NOT let it touch the bottom of the pan.

8. Cook the syrup until the thermometer reads 305°F - no stirring required.

9. Turn the heat off and stir the butter in.

10. Stir the cream mixture in carefully but take care - the mixture will begin bubbling, and it will steam quite dramatically.

11. Continue to stir, running the spatula over the sides and bottom of the pan until the cream has been thoroughly incorporated and the whole sauce is smooth.

12. Adjust the heat to where the mixture boils vigorously - but not too violently. Cook, occasionally stirring, until the thermometer reads 225°F. If you prefer your sauce to thicken like hot fudge, continue to 228°F.

13. Pour the sauce into a heatproof jar for storage.

14. Before you need to use it, gently reheat it in the microwave or a pan until it is just warmed through and flows well.

This sauce is perfect over vanilla ice cream and topped off with chopped nuts. It will also keep for a long time in the refrigerator.

Herbes de Provence

Ingredients:

- 1 tbsp fennel seeds
- ¼ cup dried thyme
- 2 tbsp dried rosemary
- 3 tbsp dried marjoram
- 3 tbsp dried summer savory - optional
- 1 tbsp dried basil
- 1 tbsp dried tarragon
- 1 tsp dried chervil - optional
- 1 tsp dried culinary lavender
- 1 tsp dried mint

Instructions:

0. Using a spice grinder, grind the rosemary and fennel seeds and add them to a mixing bowl.
1. Stir in the remaining herbs.

That's it - you can store this in an airtight container and use it for seasoning chicken, meat, fish, vegetables, salads, stews, and soups.

How to Use

Add Herbes de Provence before or during the cooking process, never after. It can be used for flavoring vinaigrettes, as a steak rub, as part of the base for tomato sauce. You can also add it to salt and olive oil to coat chicken breasts - simply marinate the chicken for one hour and grill it. You can season chicken thighs with the skin on in the same way and braise them with tomatoes, white wine, and shallots cut in half.

How to Store Herbes de Provence

Herbes de Provence should be stored in an airtight container, like a glass mason jar. Stored correctly, they will last from six months to a year, depending on how fresh the herbs were to begin with. They should be stored somewhere dry and cool, away from heat or light sources. You can also store them in colored glass jars to help keep light out.

Is There a Difference between Herbes de Provence and Italian Seasoning?

Yes. Some recipes will allow you to swap these for one another, but they do have their differences. The obvious difference is where they originate - Herbes de Provence originated in the South of France because the herbs grow there naturally. At the same time, Italian seasoning includes herbs that are typically used in Italian cuisine. However, it is worth noting - and it may disappoint you to learn it - that Italian seasoning is not of Italian origin; it was invented in America.

Because Italy and France are so close to one another, they share some of the same herbs, like rosemary, thyme, and oregano. However, Herbes de Provence is genuinely French (not American) and has a much longer list of ingredients.

Traditionally, lavender was never included in that list, but it is being added to homemade versions more and more. It adds a stronger taste and aroma and pairs well with certain dishes, such as lamb. If you don't want lavender on every dish you use it in, make two batches, one with and one without.

Chapter 9: Creating Lavender Oil and Essential Oil

Essential oils are a big thing these days, with many uses, but not everyone knows how to use them properly. Undoubtedly, you have heard the term "carrier oil" in conjunction with essential oils, so before we dive into the topic and look at how you can make your own lavender oils, we need to look at what these oils are and how they differ from essential oils.

Carrier Oils

A carrier oil is a vegetable oil derived from a plant's fatty parts, like the kernel, nut, or seed. They are an important oil because they are vital for diluting the essential oils you use on your skin. In fact, there is a reason they are called carrier oils, and I'm sure you can guess what it is - they carry the oils into your skin. Typically, these are heavy oils, and either don't have a smell or have a slightly nutty smell.

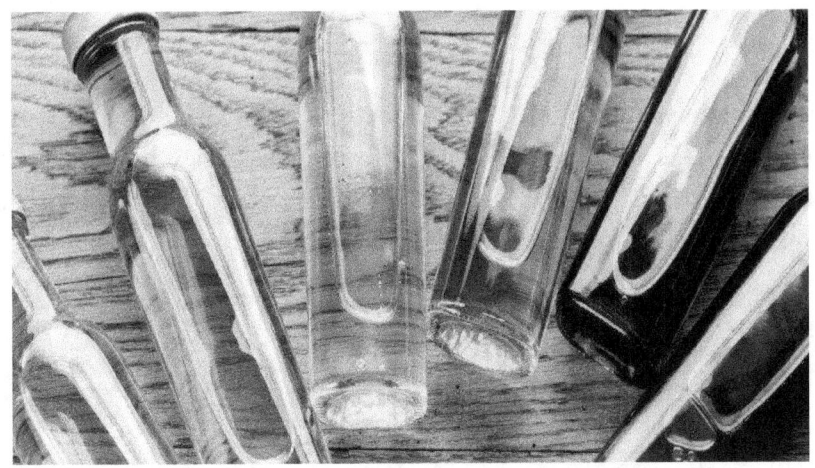

They differ from essential oils because they don't leave a heavy aroma on the body, nor do they evaporate. They are commonly used in topical applications because they are moisturizing and contain important, healthy plant nutrients such as minerals and fat-soluble vitamins that are good for the skin. Some of the carrier oils can even be ingested in their natural form. The best carrier oils to use are cold-pressed and stored in dark glass bottles with tight-fitting lids. Where a mixture only requires one or two drops of essential oils, you would use larger volumes of the carrier oils because they don't have such strong potency.

Essential Oils

Essential oils are taken from the roots, bark, leaves, and other parts of plants and are not as viscous as carrier oils. They have a much stronger aroma and are incredibly potent, so, as with using dried lavender in cooking, a little does go a long way.

On their own, essential oils are concentrated and may irritate the skin. That is one reason a carrier oil should always be used with essential oils, diluting them before you put them on your skin. And, before you use any oil for the first time, put a small amount on your skin, just to make sure you don't have a reaction to it. Some people are highly allergic to some essential oils, so it's better to be safe than sorry.

Essential oils will not spoil if they are stored correctly, and a couple of drops diluted in carrier oil is usually more than sufficient.

The Takeaway

The biggest difference between essential and carrier oils is that the latter dilute the former and transfer them to your skin, and, according to age, the dilution percentage will vary. Carrier oils are a kind of support system, ensuring you can use the essential oils efficiently.

Lavender Essential Oil

There is no doubt that lavender essential oil is one of the most popular, not to mention one of the most versatile oils for aromatherapy. The oil is distilled from the English lavender varieties, Lavandula Angustifolia. It is used for promoting sleep and relaxation and is firmly believed to be useful in treating fungal infections, anxiety, eczema, menstrual cramps, nausea, depression, and allergies.

In terms of using essential oils, lavender is classed as multipurpose, reported to have useful properties, such as:

- Anti-fungal
- Anti-depressant
- Anti-inflammatory

- Antibacterial
- Antiseptic
- Antispasmodic
- Antimicrobial
- Analgesic
- Sedative
- Hypotensive
- Detoxifying

The Benefits of Lavender Oil

Lavender oil is one of the most widely studied in terms of its properties, and the research has found this:

• It Soothes the Nervous System

Studies have shown that inhaling lavender oil mixtures can soothe and calm the nervous system. This makes it one of the best alternative remedies for anxiety, stress, fatigue, and depression.

• It Relieves Nausea

Studies also show that inhaling the scent of lavender can help relieve motion sickness and nausea.

• It Eases Headaches

Inhaling lavender scent or massaging lavender oil into your forehead, temples, neck, and behind the ears can help relieve headaches.

• It Can Help You Sleep

Just adding a drop or two of lavender oil to a diffuser in your bedroom or on your pillow can help relax your body and mind, promoting better sleep.

- **It Can Help Heal Minor Wounds**

Dilute lavender oil with distilled water and apply it to minor wounds. This helps the cells regenerate faster and promotes healing.

- **It Can Help Alleviate Menstrual Cramps**

Massaging lavender oil into the abdomen during the menstrual cycle can help relieve cramping and pain.

- **It Can Help to Nourish Your Skin**

Lavender is full of antioxidants that help nourish and protect your skin, making it the ideal addition for any skincare regime.

- **It Can Help Hydrate Sore, Chapped Lips**

Mixing lavender and coconut oil make the ideal balm to soothe and hydrate chapped lips.

- **It Can Help Prevent Cold Sores**

Because lavender has anti-fungal and antimicrobial properties, it can help stop cold sores from forming.

- **It Helps Combat Acne**

Again, because of its antimicrobial and antibacterial properties, lavender oil is a great solution for treating acne and helping keep outbreaks away.

- **It Can Help Minimize Sunspots**

When you use a lavender oil formula consistently, it can help to reduce the chances of sunspots appearing.

- **It Can Help Relieve Itchy Skin**

Because lavender has anti-inflammatory properties, it can help relieve inflammation and itching caused by insect bites, sunburn, and eczema.

- **It Can Help Reduce or Eliminate Dandruff**

A mixture of lavender oil and olive oil massaged into the scalp can help relieve scalp imbalances and eliminate dandruff.

- **It Can Help Stimulate Hair Growth**

Lavender is also known to stimulate blood circulation, and when applied to the scalp, mixed with olive oil, it can stimulate hair growth.

Warning

You may see, on the internet, some sources saying you can add lavender oil to your mascara, and it will strengthen, volumize, and lengthen your eyelashes. Please do NOT do this. Using concentrated lavender oil near your eyes is a sure recipe for disaster, and there is no research to back those claims up. You shouldn't even use diluted lavender oil near or on your eyes.

- **It's a Great Fragrance**

Lavender scent is clean, refreshing, and floral, making it one of the best choices to use as a fragrance.

Potential Side Effects

Please read this carefully - lavender oil can irritate the skin or cause an allergic reaction in some people. You must stop using lavender oil straight away if you experience headaches, vomiting, or nausea.

Lavender oil can also be toxic, so it is not recommended to ingest it unless a trained medical professional supervises it.

Dosage and Preparation

Unlike many things, lavender oil doesn't come with any recommended daily allowances. The aromatherapy principles say that simply breathing the scent in or massaging the oil into your skin sends a message to your limbic system. This is a region in the brain that influences your nervous system and plays a big part in regulating emotions.

One of the most popular approaches involves a combination of lavender and a carrier oil, such as sweet almond or jojoba. When lavender oil is combined with a carrier oil, you can add it to your bath or massage it into your skin.

Lavender oil can also be sprinkled on a tissue or cloth and inhaled or added to a vaporizer or diffuser.

What to Look For

The FDA does not regulate essential oils, and there are no purity standards, either. When purchasing your essential oils, try to find suppliers who distill their own oils or who only deal with reputable distillers. They should also analyze the product's quality using GC/MS (gas chromatography and mass spectrometry).

When you purchase pure lavender oil, make sure the label contains the correct Latin name - Lavandula angustifolia. There should be no other ingredients or oils listed on the label. If you see another, like sweet almond oil, jojoba oil, fractionated coconut oil, etc., you know the oil has been diluted and is not suitable for use in diffusers.

Essential oils should also be stored away from the light and packaged in cobalt or dark amber bottles.

Lavender may be touted as helping to soothe anxiety, but it should never be used as a replacement for professional medical or mental health treatment. No matter how mild your anxiety order may be, always seek your doctor's advice before using any essential oils, especially if you are constantly fatigued, always worrying, struggle to sleep, and have a rapid heartbeat.

While lavender oil can be used undiluted for some things, it is often best used when it has been diluted, and here are some ways you can do that.

1. Using a Carrier Oil

Add your carrier oil to a dark glass bottle, almost filling it. If your bottle is an 8 oz bottle, start by adding one teaspoon of lavender essential oil. As you get used to it, you can increase it gradually to two tablespoons, but no more. You can use this as a moisturizer, massage oil, or bath oil. To use it in your bath, add one ounce of the oil to the running water to ensure it mixes thoroughly.

2. Using Cold Water

Fill an 8 oz spray bottle with cold water and add five to ten drops of lavender oil. You can use this mixture to freshen a room, spray on your bedding, or anywhere you want to smell of lavender.

3. Using Hot Water

Pour two cups of boiling water into a container and add five to ten drops of lavender oil. Lean over the bowl until your nose is about 12 inches away, and inhale it. Steam aromatherapy is great for helping asthma and reducing stuffiness associated with colds and flu.

Tip

When you mix your lavender oils, how strong it is will depend on what you want it for. Stronger mixes are suitable for massages and pain relief, while relaxation requires a weaker mix.

How to Make Your Own Lavender Oil

If you grow plenty of lavender in your garden, you can turn it into your own healing, fabulous-smelling oil. It is so easy to make lavender oil at home with whole dried lavender buds. While it won't be so concentrated as the pure oils you can buy, you can still incorporate it into your health, beauty, and home routines. Lavender is one of the best all-around oils, known for its soothing, healing properties.

Shortly, I'll provide you with the steps to make your own oil, but first, some questions need answering.

What Kind of Lavender is Best for Making Lavender Oil?

You can use any lavender to make oil, but the best is organically grown lavender. The best lavender for medicinal and edible uses is true English lavender, and if you are planning to cook with it, English and hybrid lavenders are the best.

Technically, French and Spanish lavender is edible, but they have a more herbaceous taste and, because they have a higher camphor content, they are somewhat more buttery. However, camphor is one of the best terpenes to help ease itching, swelling, and pain.

All lavender species contain antibacterial, anti-inflammatory, and anti-anxiety properties.

More significant than the type of lavender used to make oil is the quality and condition of the flowers. Lavender oil can be made only using completely dry flower buds. If the flowers are minutely damp, the moisture can spoil the oil and turn it moldy. By making sure they are 100% dry, you can also ensure the maximum amount of oil because, as we all know, oil and water simply do not mix.

The flowers should be harvested at the right time when they are early in their blooming time. Drying the flowers should be done at low heat or by air drying; any other method will affect how much oil you can obtain from them.

What Kinds of Carrier Oils Should Be Used for Making Lavender Oil?

That will depend on what you are using it for. To use it for cooking, baking, etc., you should use edible carrier oils. But, if you want your lavender oil for use on your skin, think about the oils most compatible with your skin type, especially if you are using it on your face.

For those who don't think you should use oil on your face, you couldn't be more wrong. Look at the ingredients on your traditional moisturizer and compare it to the ingredients in your lavender oil - which one would you prefer smoothing over your skin? Then consider how much you use. A blob of chemical-laden cream or a couple of drops of natural oil?

Despite many people believing the contrary to be true, using oil in your face does not leave your skin even more oily, nor does it cause acne breakouts. Many products are touted as claiming to reduce the shine on your face or remove acne, but they do nothing more than strip all the natural oils from your skin and cause irritation. Not all do this, to be fair, but many do, and when the skin is stripped of natural oil, it dries out. Then it has to overcompensate for this by producing even more sebum, and that WILL make your skin exceedingly greasy.

By contrast, natural oils nourish your skin, soothe it, and restore its balance and moisture. When you add lavender or other healing ingredients, those oils can be wonderful on dry, stressed, or damaged skin, especially for those prone to blemishes and acne.

Which Carrier Oil is Best?

There are plenty of carrier oils, and they are all different. We're going to look at ten of the very best oils, but no matter which one you chose, ensure it is cold-pressed, unrefined, and of high quality. Even better, try to get oils certified as organic.

All oils are given a rating of one to five on the comedogenic scale. Oils at the low end of the scale are called non-comedogenic, which means they will not clog up your pores. Those in the middle are somewhat likely to, and those at the top end of the scale will most likely clog your pores. All oils have high levels of essential omega fatty acids, useful for nourishing, rejuvenating, and hydrating your skin. You can also mix a couple of oils to create your own custom blend.

1. Grapeseed Oil

Properties - Antimicrobial

Comedogenic Scale - 1

Grapeseed oil is a lightweight oil good for helping reduce acne. It is not greasy and easily absorbed, although it isn't as moisturizing as some other oils in this list. It is edible at room temperature or cold but cannot be used for cooking at high heat.

2. Jojoba Oil

Properties – anti-inflammatory

Comedogenic Scale – 2

Jojoba oil is another lightweight oil, non-greasy and highly absorbable, with a chemical structure much like that of human skin. It helps to break excess sebum down and reduce it, making it perfect for those with combination or oily skin. When you use this oil for the first time, you may get a rash, but this is no bad thing. The oil is busy unclogging all your pores and getting rid of the impurities in your skin. It has a long shelf-life, up to five years, but is not edible at any temperature.

3. Rosehip Seed Oil

Comedogenic Scale – 2

High in fatty acids, vitamin A, and vitamin E, rosehip seed oil helps increase the cell turnover in your skin. It can help heal scars and reduces fine lines and skin discoloration. A lightweight oil, it is easily absorbed, has a short shelf-life of up to six months, and is not for internal use.

4. Extra Virgin Olive Oil

Comedogenic Scale – 2

Extra virgin olive oil, otherwise known as EVOO, is a hydrating oil great for nourishing the skin. It is thicker than many oils and is edible at cold, room, and high heat cooking temperatures, making it a great all-purpose oil. If your skin is prone to acne, too much olive oil can cause breakouts. It contains hydroxytyrosol, a rare antioxidant that helps protect against damage from free radicals, and is also considered anti-aging.

5. Avocado Oil

Comedogenic Scale - 3

Avocado oil is one of the thickest and is quite oily but is an excellent moisturizer. It can help reduce inflammation, scars, and age spots while helping to soften the skin. It is an edible oil.

6. Coconut Oil

Properties – antiviral, antibacterial, anti-inflammatory, anti-fungal

Comedogenic Scale – 4

Coconut oil is one of the best oils in the world of natural beauty. Although it is high on the comedogenic scale, it is highly moisturizing, and one compound it contains is caprylic acid. However, virgin coconut oil is difficult to use for most infusions. At room temperature, it tends to be solid, and being high on the scale, it does clog the pores. On the other hand, fractionated coconut oil stays liquid at room temperature, making it perfect for infusions and is not as likely to clog up your pores.

7. Hemp Seed Oil

Comedogenic Scale – 0

A zero on the scale, hempseed oil is one of the lightest, driest oils and is incredibly absorbable. This is because it has a similar fat and amino acid profile as the natural oils in our skin, making it the best choice for all skin types. It can help reduce fines lines, inflammation, and acne, and it is edible.

8. Argan Oil

Comedogenic Scale – 0

Argan oil is also called Moroccan oil and is one of the most moisturizing and gentle oils. It is commonly found in beauty products, especially hair care, and when used on the skin, it can help reduce fine lines, prevent damage from the sun, soften the skin, reduce excess oil, and may even be useful for treating stretch marks. Argan oil comes in two types – edible and cosmetic-only.

9. Safflower Oil

Comedogenic Scale – 0

A good choice for irritated, dry skin and oily skin prone to acne, safflower oil is gentle, lightweight, but healing and very moisturizing. It helps to unclog pores and balance levels of natural oil in the skin. However, there is a warning – if you are allergic to the ragweed family, you should not use this oil. It is edible at high and low temperatures.

10. Sunflower Seed Oil

Like safflower oil in its properties, sunflower oil has a very high level of vitamin E, one of the most powerful antioxidants to help reduce damage from free radicals and help repair or reduce skin damage. In terms of its comedogenic rating, note that sunflower oil is available in low, moderate, or high oleic acid content - the lower the content, the lower the rating. Sunflower seed oil is edible at any heat.

How to Make Lavender Infused Oil

This is what you really wanted to know - *how to make your own lavender oil.*

Step One

Fill a half-pint or pint jar at least three-quarters full of lavender buds or flowers - 100% dried. You can use smaller or larger jars if you want; it depends on how much you want to make. Be aware that the size of the container you choose dictates the amount of oil you make.

Step Two

Pour your carrier oil over the dried flowers, making sure there is enough oil to fully submerge the flowers, allowing them to move in the oil freely. Seal it with a tight lid. You can use one oil or two for this - one of the best blends is olive and almond oil.

Step Three

Leave the jar somewhere warm and sunny between one and three weeks to allow the flowers time to infuse in the oil. Try to remember to shake it occasionally. Lavender will float in the oil, so it should be gently turned and shaken to mix it all up, especially during the first week. The best place is a warm sunny windowsill or a room with bright ambient lighting. Do not allow the oil to get excessively hot.

Step Four

The lavender oil can now be strained into a bowl. Line a fine-mesh strainer with a reusable nut bag or cheesecloth and pour the oil through. When it has strained through, gently wring the bag or cloth to get the last drops of oil out and discard the flowers.

That's all there is to making your own lavender-infused oil. This is not as strong as pure essential oils, which means you don't have to dilute it so much. Simply dilute it, using one method listed earlier, to your chosen level.

Storage and Shelf Life

The finished oil should be stored in a clean container, preferably glass, with a tight lid. Keep it somewhere cool, dry, and dark. Shelf-life depends on what carrier oil/s you use and the condition of your flowers.

The label on your carrier oil bottle will indicate the optimum shelf-life – some oils will turn rancid quicker than others, but most will last an average of one to two years, provided they are stored correctly. You can extend this by storing yours in the refrigerator.

9 Ways to Use Lavender Oil

Now that you have made your oil, what are you going to use it for? Here are nine ways you can use it:

1. Healing Moisturizer

Lavender is well-known for helping heal acne, and a little will go quite a long way. A few drops are more than enough to avoid leaving an oily sheen across your skin. Spread it over your skin evenly and massage it in lightly.

2. Oil Cleanser

If you are not aware of the OCM - oil cleansing method - it is very much like washing your face but using oil rather than soap. Put several drops of the oil onto your fingers and lather your face up— massage for 30 seconds to a minute. Heat a washcloth - use hot water - and lay it over your face for 30 seconds. The pores in your skin open, and impurities are drawn out. Rinse the cloth out and do it again. Last, use a damp towel to wipe off the excess oil.

3. Topical Application

Lavender oil isn't just good for your face. You can use it as an all-over body moisturizer, as a massage oil, for skin scrapes, bites, eczema, sunburn, rashes, scars, and more. And if you own a set of essential oil rollers, add some oil to them to roll on your temples, neck, and wrists at night, just before you go to bed.

4. Skincare Product Ingredient

Lots of homemade skincare recipes include oil, so you can use your lavender oil in body butter, ointments, salves, soaps, and much more. You will find recipes for some of these in the last chapter.

5. As a Hair Care Product

While oil probably shouldn't be used daily to condition your hair, your lavender infusion can occasionally be used as a deep conditioner. Lavender has also been shown to strengthen hair growth too. Apply the oil in an even coat to your hair and massage it into your scalp. Leave it for between 15 minutes and three hours, and then wash it out using your normal shampoo.

6. As a Makeup Remover

Oil is fantastic for removing makeup because it draws impurities out while reducing inflammation and redness and targeting acne. Please do not get it into contact with your eyes.

7. As a Marinade

Lavender is one of the popular herbs used in baked goods and meat marinades. If your recipe calls for oil, swap some or all of it for lavender oil, providing you used edible carrier oil. In this way, when you ingest lavender, it provides your immune system with a boost, fights bacterial and fungal infections, and helps reduce inflammation.

8. In Cleaning Products

Homemade sprays often require oil to help make your stainless-steel surfaces shine. When you make cleaning sprays using citrus and vinegar, add a couple of tablespoons of your infused oil. Best used in the bathroom and kitchen, lavender oil cuts through odors and is a natural antibacterial. However, citrus/vinegar mixes should not be used on granite, stone, or marble surfaces.

9. As a Gift

If you want, you can make a large batch of oil, pour it into small containers, make some nice labels and give it as a gift to someone special.

Various Lavender Oil Blends

To finish, here are some lavender blends you can make yourself using essential oils.

Good Sleep Blend

Ingredients:

- 1 drop of chamomile essential oil
- 9 drops of lavender essential oil
- 3 drops of vetiver or neroli essential oil
- 2 drops of sweet orange essential oil

You can use these oils in electric or reed diffusers or a spray bottle. However, depending on the method you use, the water-to-oil ratios will be different. The steps below are for an easy spray bottle method:

Instructions:
1. Add the oils to a spray bottle.
2. Add 2 oz or 60 ml of distilled water.
3. Shake well to combine it all thoroughly and spray over your pillow or bedsheets just before you go to bed.

And this blend is for an electric diffuser:

Ingredients:
- 4 drops of lavender essential oil
- 3 drops of bergamot essential oil

OR

- 4 drops of lavender essential oil
- 1 drop of bergamot essential oil
- 1 drop of patchouli essential oil

- 1 drop of ylang-ylang essential oil

Instructions:

Simply add all the ingredients of your chosen blend to an electric diffuser.

Massage Blends

Lavender essential oil is ideal for relieving pain, including indigestion pain, muscle pain, bloating, wounds, backache, joint pain, muscle aches, and sprains. When you dilute the oil with a carrier oil and massage it into the abdomen, it can help stimulate movement in the intestines needed to get the gastric juices flowing to aid digestion. In turn, this relieves vomiting, flatulence, nausea, diarrhea, and stomach pain. And inhaling a lavender-infused massage oil can also relieve emotional pain that comes with depression and stress, promoting mental relaxation.

Here are two blends you can try:

Stress Relief

Ingredients:

- 7 tbsp of grape seed, avocado, or sweet almond carrier oil
- 5 drops of bergamot essential oil
- 4 drops of mandarin essential oil
- 4 drops of lavender essential oil
- 3 drops of lemongrass essential oil

Instructions:

1. Blend the essential oils in a PET plastic bottle or dark glass jar.
2. Add the carrier oil to dilute it.
3. Massage it into your chest for penetrating and comforting warmth.

Muscle Pain

Ingredients:

- 4 tbsp of your choice of carrier oil
- 2 drops of lavender essential oil
- 2 drops of rosemary essential oil

Instructions

1. Blend the essential oils in a dark glass jar or PET plastic bottle.
2. Add the carrier oil to dilute it and shake well.
3. Massage into the body gently to relieve pain.

Bath Blends

When you add lavender oil to a bath, its antimicrobial properties kick into gear and stimulate your immune function. This helps combat harm caused by contaminants by stopping bacteria from growing or reproducing.

Inhaling lavender-infused bath water helps relieve inflammation that causes headaches, sinus problems, and pain. And because it has expectorant and decongestant properties, it is perfect for relieving coughs, the flu, colds, and other respiratory issues. It loosens mucus and phlegm in the throat and nose, making it easier to eliminate them from your body. Plus, it can help battle respiratory infections and inflammation caused by tonsillitis, laryngitis, bronchitis, and other inflammatory conditions with its antibacterial properties.

When you add Epsom salts to a bath, it can boost your circulation and pep up an aching, tired body, relieve abdominal cramps, inflamed joints, and pain. Adding lavender helps ease tension in the body and headaches caused by the tension and relieves sore, tired feet. Epsom salts and lavender are also proven to help aid in digestion and detoxify the body.

Here are two blends that can help you:

Pain and Cold Relief

Ingredients:

- 125 ml of sweet almond or jojoba carrier oil
- 10 drops of lavender essential oil
- 5 drops of frankincense essential oil
- 5 drops of marjoram essential oil
- 1 drop of cedarwood essential oil

Instructions:

1. Blend all the ingredients in a PET plastic or dark glass bottle.
2. Add to a warm running bath and stir the oils in.
3. Enjoy a long soak!

The remaining oils should be stored away from the bathroom in a dark, cool place. Bathrooms are too humid and can affect the oil's efficacy and lead to it spoiling early.

Bath Salts for Aches and Pains

Ingredients:

- A square of cheesecloth or muslin, 10 x 10 inch
- 1 cup of dried lavender buds
- 20 drops of lavender essential oil
- 1 cup of Dead Sea salt or Epsom salt
- ½ cup of baking soda – optional
- Enough yarn or string to tie around a small bag

Instructions:

1. Put the lavender buds in the middle of the cloth or muslin.
2. Add the lavender essential oil, one drop at a time.
3. Gather the materials up loosely in the cloth and tie them into a pouch.
4. Hang it from the bath taps and run the water – the pouch should hang into the water.
5. Add the salts and soda, ensuring they are fully dissolved in the water.

Cosmetic and Beauty Use

When you use lavender oil in lotions, creams, or facial steams, it helps unclog your skin, detoxify it, brightens and tone it. Its antibacterial and anti-inflammatory properties also help it treat acne and reduce itching. If you use it in a facial steam, the steam will help decongestion caused by cold, flu, or allergies. The aroma also reduces fatigue and anxiety, and stress and leaves your home smelling cool and clean.

Lavender oil also has cicatrizing properties, which add moisture to the skin and soothes dry skin, cuts, burns, and other wounds or damage. And it has anti-aging properties that help smooth over wrinkles, boosts your circulation, nourishes, and oxygenates the skin, helping it look and feel rejuvenated and healthy.

Lavender Facial Steam

Ingredients:

- 3 cups of distilled water
- 4 drops of lavender essential oil
- 3 drops of geranium oil

Instructions:

1. Cleanse your skin thoroughly.

2. Boil the water, remove it from the heat and pour it into a bowl; leave for 5 minutes to cool.

3. Add the oils and stir them in.

4. Put the bowl on a stable surface, and put a large towel over your shoulders, head, and bowl.

5. Lean over it, keeping your face about 10 to 12 inches away.

6. Close your eyes and inhale deeply.

7. Relax, ensuring your eyes are closed for the entire team – the oils can irritate your eyes.

Lavender oil is also known to reduce hair loss, partly due to having sedative and anti-depressant properties. You might ask how these can help your hair, but they alleviate the depression, anxiety, stress, and insomnia commonly associated with hair conditioning and loss. Adding lavender oil to natural shampoos and massaging it regularly into your scalp will boost circulation, enhance hair condition and growth, treat dandruff, and help strengthen your hair while improving your mindset.

Lavender Oil Conditioning Shampoo

Ingredients:

- 100 ml of shampoo (natural if you can get it)
- 10 drops of sandalwood essential oil
- 6 drops of lavender essential oil
- 4 drops of ylang-ylang essential oil

Instructions

1. Using a dark, clean container, mix all the ingredients together.
2. Dab a small amount on your hair and lather it up, massaging it into your scalp.
3. Repeat if needed, then condition and rinse your hair.

Herbs and Oils to Help Your Hair

Sometimes, your hair needs a little more help, especially when you are stressed or if the weather has turned harsh. These oils are ideal to use to make your own hot-oil treatments. Simply choose your carrier and your essential oils and follow the instructions:

Carrier Oils:

- **Argan oil** - suits all hair types, including fine hair
- **Avocado oil** – suits dry hair. This is heavy oil, so blend a little glycerin or lighter carrier oil with it
- **Coconut oil** – suits greasy hair
- **Jojoba oil** – suits all hair types, including fine hair
- **Oat oil** – ideal for treating seborrhea. Another heavy oil should be blended with a little glycerin or light carrier oil
- **Olive oil** – suits dark hair. It's a heavy oil that should be blended with glycerin or other oils.

For the heavy oils, you only need to blend a small amount with the other oils.

Essential Oils:

- **Chamomile** – suits blond hair and fine hair
- **Chili** – ideal for hair loss
- **Cinnamon bark** – suits auburn and red hair
- **Clove bud** – suits auburn hair
- **Lavender** – suits all hair types
- **Rosemary** – suits gray hair going thin and dark hair
- **Sage** – suits dark hair
- **Thyme** – suits dark hair

Instructions:

1. Heat four tablespoons of your chosen carrier oil gently.

2. Take it off the heat and add 30 drops of your chosen essential oils – use one or a blend, depending on what you want.

3. Massage the oil into your hair sparingly, with your focus on the ends of your hair. If your scalp is dry, massage the oil into it.

4. Wrap plastic wrap around your hair and then wrap in a towel.

5. Leave it on for at least one hour.

6. Wash it out, shampooing thoroughly.

7. Repeat the shampoo if needed, and then condition your hair.

If you have any oil left, store it in a clean container in the refrigerator.

Chapter 10: Lavender Scented Gifts

Handmade gifts are always better than store-bought, for the simple reason that more thought has gone into them and, usually, a lot of hard work and love. Homemade gifts are unique, and the recipient can see how much has gone into them.

Some of the best homemade gifts involve using essential oils or herbs, and lavender is one of the most popular. It has a calming effect and can be incorporated into many items, including body and bath gifts.

Making lavender gifts requires dried lavender and/or lavender essential oil, and you can find pretty much everything you need in gift and craft shops.

Without further ado, here are some of the nicest gifts you can make and give using lavender.

Lavender Bath Bombs

Fizzy bath bombs are the best way to enjoy a bath, and when you make them using lavender, you get to enjoy the most relaxing, stress-relieving bath you will ever have, plus one of the most fragrant.

And guess what? You don't even need to splash out on special bath bomb molds - lots of other things will work. Two-part Christmas decorations that snap together are ideal, and you can buy these in craft stores, but if you can't find one, don't worry.

There is nothing to say that your bath bombs must be round - you can use chocolate molds that come in all sizes and shapes but, if you have your heart set on round ones, cut a tennis ball in half. Or you can use ice-cube trays, silicone muffin liners, shot glasses, and so on - use your imagination and create some wild and wonderful shapes and sizes.

You Will Need:

- A mixing bowl - metal or glass work best
- Silicon spatula
- whisk
- Protective gloves
- Your bath bomb molds

Metal and glass mixing bowls work the best because plastic tends to absorb the smell from the essential oils.

Ingredients:

- 1 cup of baking soda
- ½ cup of citric acid
- ½ a cup of Epsom salts
- 1 to 2 tbsp of dried lavender flowers

- 3 tsp of almond oil
- 5 drops of lavender essential oil
- 5 drops of eucalyptus essential oil
- Purple pigment powder or soap colorant
-

Notes

Baking soda is also sold under the name of bicarbonate of soda and can be found in the baking section of your local grocery store.

The oil makes your bath bombs give off a moisturizing feel. However, if your gift recipient has nut allergies, do NOT use almond oil – try olive oil instead.

If you want your bath bombs to be colorful and can't find soap pigment, add food coloring. The basic colors of red, blue, and yellow can be mixed to give you any color you want. For lavender, you probably want purple ones, so use red and blue. However, when you first mix it, it will be green but, as it sets, it turns purple.

Citric Acid

You may be wondering where to get citric acid from. You can buy it online or in the canning or baking section of your local supermarket. If you can't find it, there is another way to do this using cream of tartar. However, you only need half the amount, so, where the recipe says 1 cup of citric acid, use half a cup of cream of tartar, which can also be found in the grocery store baking section.

What Not to Use

Some people try to use alternative ingredients, and while this may work to a certain extent in baking, it won't work for this kind of recipe. Here are two ingredients you should never use when making bath bombs:

Borax

Please, never use borax or sodium borate in anything like this. It is used as an ant poison and is toxic to the kidneys and liver when ingested. It has even been proven to cause liver cancer. While you may not be drinking the bathwater, you probably don't want to be bathing in borax.

Corn flour

While corn flour may make the water and your skin feel soft, it will also feed yeast infections. You may not have one but, I wouldn't take the chance of bathing in it.

What to Do

Step One

Add the dry ingredients - citric acid, Epsom salts, and baking soda - to a bowl and mix it using a whisk. You can also add the color pigment here (not the food coloring)

Step Two

Whisk the dried flowers into the mixture.

Step Three

Combine the essential oils in a small bowl and add them to the dry mixture, a little bit at a time. Whisk them in - if you add too much, the mixture will start foaming and fizzing. When all your oils are mixed in, the consistency should be like wet sand. If it isn't, add the tiniest amount of water and whisk - repeat until you get the right consistency. At this stage, add your food coloring if that's what you are using.

Step Four

Fill your bath bomb molds full and pack the mixture in. If you are using the two-part decorations, slightly overfill each side and push them together, scraping off any overflow. Leave the molds for a few minutes to allow the bombs to start hardening off.

Step Five

Remove the bombs from the molds and leave them somewhere warm and dry (not in full sunlight) to dry for a couple of hours. Try nestling them in tissue paper – this stops the bottoms from flaking off and helps with the drying process.

Once your bath bombs are made, they should be used within a couple of weeks; otherwise, they may lose their fizziness.

Lavender Infused Oil

Lavender-infused oil is perfect for wiping over bug bites, massaging into tired, restless legs, massaging into a dry, flaky scalp, and a base ingredient in many other recipes, like salves, creams, soaps, and so on. Making it is simple, and provided you store it correctly, it will last for between nine and twelve months.

What You Need:

- A half-liter jar with a tight lid - mason or canning jars work well
- Dried or fresh lavender
- 250 ml of carrier oil - see below

This will make 160 ml of oil.

Note

Your choice of carrier oil is important as you need to consider many things - composition, aroma, contraindications, price, shelf-life, and benefits. You also need to know what its absorbency rate is. Some carrier oils are fast-absorbing and don't leave your skin covered in a greasy sheen, while others are slower and leave a slightly oily sheen.

I prefer to use grapeseed oil for this:

- It has a fast rate of absorption.
- It has no scent and is an ecological oil with lots of antioxidants.
- It helps fight damage from free radicals, is anti-aging, and can help heal skin exposed to the elements.
- It contains resveratrol, and vitamins A, C and E.
- It contains polyphenols that are linked to preventing cancer and aging.

- It is a light oil, rich in nutrients, and perfect for all skin types.

What to Do

How to prepare your oil:

1. Pack your jar with dried lavender
2. Add your oil, making sure the flowers are covered

Now, you can do it in one of three ways:

1. Cover your jar with breathable canvas and leave it somewhere warm and dry (not in direct sunlight) for a couple of weeks. Then, use a soft cloth over a sieve and pour the oil through. Use the cloth to grind it; ensure you only get pure oil and no bits of the flower.

2. Leave the jar uncovered and put it in a small pan with a few inches of water. Gently heat the water for a few hours on low heat, ensuring the water doesn't evaporate, and then strain the oil.

3. Put the lid on the jar and place it in a dark cupboard for four to six weeks. Occasionally shake it, and when the time has passed, strain the oil.

Lavender Salve

For this, you can use the lavender-infused oil you made. This salve works well on tired muscles, restless legs, and massaged on the back of the neck and temples to relieve headaches. And, because it helps condition the skin, it's also great for small dry spots.

What You Need:

- 100 g (3 ½ oz.) of your lavender-infused oil
- 15 g (1/2 oz.) beeswax
- An empty tin can or heatproof jar

If you prefer to make a vegan variation, use candelilla wax in place of beeswax. You will need roughly half the amount, so about 7 ½ g.

What to Do:

Step One

Place your can or jar in a saucepan with a couple of inches of water.

Step Two

Add the wax and oil and heat on medium-low until the wax has melted fully.

Step Three

You can add a couple of drops of lavender essential oil if you want to, but this is optional.

Step Four

Pour the mixture into a jar or tin.

Stored properly, it will last from nine to twelve months.

Lavender and Honey Hand Scrub

This wonderful scrub is great for exfoliating your skin, leaving it smooth, silky, and soft. It works especially well on the knees, elbows, and feet.

What You Need

- ½ a cup of cane sugar
- 1 to 2 tbsp of lavender-infused oil
- 1 tsp of organic honey
- A couple of drops of lavender essential oil

What to Do:

Step One

Mix all the ingredients thoroughly in a bowl. You may need to play around with the amount of oil and sugar to get the right consistency – not too oily.

Step Two

Decant the mixture into a jar or small tin.

Scoop a small amount when needed and rub it into dry skin before rinsing with warm water. Don't make any more than you can use for a few days in a row. Otherwise, you need to consider adding preservatives.

Lavender Oatmeal Bath Tea

Lavender oatmeal bath tea is true decadence and is dead simple to make. You don't have to make it into tea bags if you don't want to; you can put it in a jar and spoon it when you want.

What You Need:

- 1 cup of Epsom salts
- 1 cup of oatmeal
- 2 tbsp of dried lavender
- 20 drops (1 ml) of lavender essential oil

This will fill a jar of approximately half a liter or six tea bags.

Equipment to Package Your Bath Salts:

- 500 ml glass jar with a lid
- Jar labels – make your own and print them onto sticky labels or buy blank ones and write on them
- Double-sided tape
- A metal tea infuser – optional

OR

- Six tea bags – size 3, you can get these on Amazon
- Cotton string/embroidery floss cut into 6-inch lengths
- Double-sided tape
- A stapler
- Labels – again, you can easily make your own

What to Do:

Step One

Measure the lavender, salts, and oatmeal into a bowl and mix them.

Step Two

Add the essential oil and stir to coat the dried ingredients - a silicone spatula or wooden spoon is best.

Step Three

If you are making a jar of salts, spoon the mixture in through a funnel or cone made of paper, fill the jar up and put the lid on. Add your labels using double-sided tape, tie a pretty ribbon around it, or do it up in any way you want. If giving as a gift, add a metal spice or tea infuser - this way, the recipient won't be bathing in oatmeal and lavender - only the water will be scented.

Step Four

If you are making the teabag method, fill the bags with the mixture and staple a piece of floss at the top - the bag can hang from the bath taps, so the water runs through it or just thrown in the bath and fished out afterward.

Use tape to put the labels on and package them up in a neat box to give as a gift.

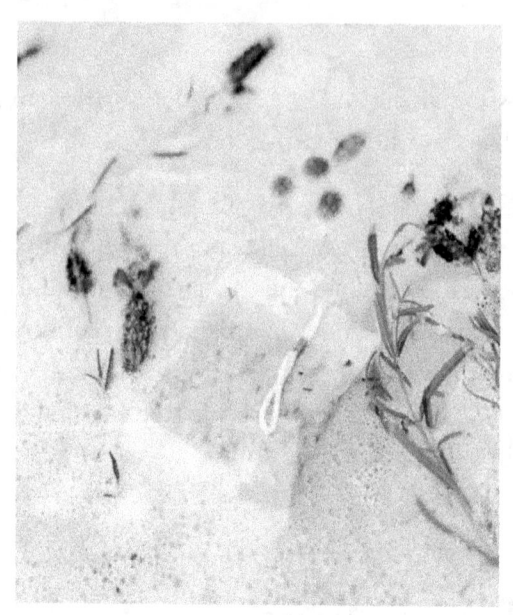

Lavender Mist for Yoga/Exercise Mats

Because lavender has antibacterial properties, it is perfect for cleaning a yoga or exercise mat after use. And the aroma will help you retain a calm state of mind, even when you are done exercising.

What You Need:

- 3 oz. of distilled water
- 1 oz. of organic witch hazel
- Three drops of lavender essential oil
- A drop or two of tea tree oil - optional
- A spray bottle, approximately 4 oz.

If you prefer not to measure your ingredients, simply use your eyes. Whatever size bottle you use, fill it three-quarters with distilled water and the rest with witch hazel before adding the essential oil.

Simply shake the container to mix it and spray it over the mat. Wipe down using a clean cloth.

Lavender Bath Salts

Bath salts are a wonderful way of relaxing your mind and muscles, especially when lavender is added.

You Will Need:

- 1 cup of salt – Epsom, Pink Himalayan, or Dead Sea – one or a combination of
- 2 tbsp of dried lavender flowers
- 10 drops of lavender essential oil
- Lidded container, such as a mason jar, approximately 8 oz.

Simply combine all the ingredients in a bowl and transfer them to the jar. Put the lid on and use it as needed. If you are giving this as a gift, consider adding a pretty ribbon and a nice label to the jar.

Lavender Diffuser Necklace

This is a wonderful gift, giving a loved one a way of having aromatherapy on the go.

You Will Need:

- 18 to 30 inches of cording or other suitable material
- A few wooden beads
- Decorative beads – optional
- 2 to 6 drops of lavender essential oil

What to Do:

Step One

Cut your cord – 18 inches if your necklace is a standard length, 30 inches for a longer one.

Step Two

String the beads onto it and tie off the ends.

Step Three

Drip the essential oil onto the beads, lightly rubbing it in. The wood will absorb the oils and give off the wonderful scent of lavender.

Lavender Dream Sachet

Tuck a lavender dream sachet beneath your pillow at night for a calm, relaxed night's sleep. These are easy to make, and you can use pre-made pouches or, if you feel creative, make your own. Keep things simple, or decorate the sachets before you fill them with lavender.

You Will Need:

- A pre-made pouch - drawstring, popper, or Velcro

OR

- Two squares of fabric, approximately 6 inches square - natural cotton is best
- Embroidery yarn
- A needle

And

- ½ to 1 cup of dried lavender flowers
- A couple of drops of lavender essential oil

Step One

If you are making your own pouch, use a whipstitch to sew the fabric together on three sides - you can use a sewing machine if you prefer.

Step Two

Almost fill your pouch - homemade or pre-made - with the lavender and add the essential oil.

Step Three

Sew or tie the bag shut.

To embroider a decoration, do it before you fill the sachet.

To use, simply squeeze it lightly, and the wonderful lavender aroma will be released.

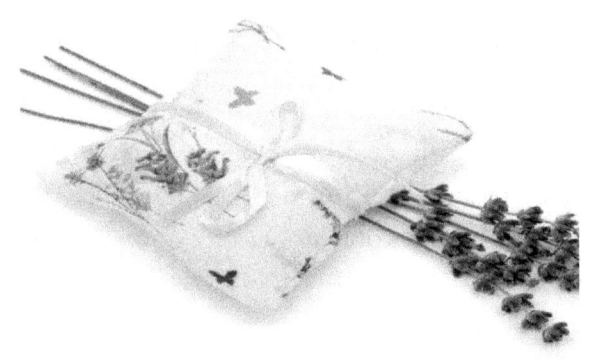

Lavender Potpourri

Lavender potpourri is wonderful on its own but if you want the scent of an English garden, add rose petals to it. You also need not use lavender essential oil for this if you don't want to, as the dried lavender will produce a strong aroma of its own. However, the oil does ensure the smell lasts for much longer.

What You Need:

- Some paper towels
- A rolling pin
- A measuring cup
- An airtight jar or a bowl
- 1 tsp of Orris root powder per cup of dried buds – this helps preserve the buds
- A couple of drops of lavender essential oil
- Dried lavender buds

What to Do

Step One

Measure out your dried lavender blooms and place them in a single layer on a paper towel. Cover with another and crush them using your rolling pin.

Step Two

Rub the individual flower heads over a cup and then add the Orris powder – 1 cup per cup of flowers. Stir it through, distributing it evenly.

Step Three

Add the lavender oil if you are using it. Rub it through, coating the blooms.

Step Four

If you are using it straight away, pour it into a bowl and place it where you want the scent. If not, put it in an airtight container until you want to use it. It is best to leave it a few days to allow the oil to infuse the flowers. Alternatively, you can fill small pouches or bags, tie them up, and give them as gifts.

Whipped Lavender Body Butter

After a soothing bath, there is no better way to moisturize your skin than to smooth whipped body butter all over. And it is easy to make and the perfect gift for a good friend who deserves a little pampering.

What You Need:

- ½ a cup of solid coconut oil
- ½ a cup of sweet almond oil
- 1 cup of shea butter
- 15 to 20 drops of lavender essential oil
- Lidded glass jars

What to Do:

Step One

Put the shea butter, almond oil, and coconut oil into a glass or metal bowl and place it over a pan of water, making a double boiler – or use a double boiler, if you have one. Melt the oils, constantly whisking until completely melted.

Step Two

Remove the oil from the heat and refrigerate it until cooled.

Step Three

When the mixture is solid, add the oils and whisk the mixture using a hand mixer until it is whipped and creamy. Spoon into jars and put airtight lids on.

Use as needed or give as gifts.

Conclusion

Lavender is easy to grow, so long as you all consider the variables, choosing the suitable cultivar for your region and for what you want to use it for. Make sure your soil is right, plant the lavender, and give it a good watering. Then, you can leave it to its own devices. Lavender is one of the few plants you need not worry about watering all the time – less is better.

Remember to prune your plants once or twice a year, and you could have an ever-growing crop of wonderful smelling lavender, year after year.

I've tried to give you lots of ideas on what you can do with your lavender, from cooking to crafting, making your own oil, and making fantastic gifts, be they for friends or yourself.

All that's left now is for you to get to it! Grow your lavender, reaping the many benefits and rewards of this amazing plant.

Here's another book by Dion Rosser that you might like

References

4 Different Ways to Use Lavender in Handmade Gifts - Willow and Sage Magazine. (n.d.). Willowandsage.com. https://willowandsage.com/4-different-ways-to-use-lavender-in-handmade-gifts/

12 Types of Lavender + Growing Info. (2019, August 19). ProFlowers Blog. https://www.proflowers.com/blog/types-of-lavender

17 Brilliant Ways to Cook with Lavender. (n.d.). Martha Stewart. Retrieved from https://www.marthastewart.com/1504965/brilliant-ways-cook-lavender

Andrychowicz, A. (2018a, May 11). *Pruning Lavender: A Step-By-Step Guide.* Get Busy Gardening. https://getbusygardening.com/pruning-lavender/

Andrychowicz, A. (2018b, July 12). *How to Care For Lavender Plants.* Get Busy Gardening. https://getbusygardening.com/lavender-plant-care/

Any Known Pests of Lavender Plants. (n.d.). Home Guides | SF Gate. Retrieved from https://homeguides.sfgate.com/known-pests-lavender-plants-38977.html

Bennett, M. (n.d.). *How to Revive a Dying Lavender Plant.* Gardener Report.com. Retrieved from https://www.gardenerreport.com/how-to-revive-a-dying-lavender-plant

Diane. (2019, November 6). *33 DIY Ideas With Lavender.* DIY Joy. https://diyjoy.com/diy-projects-lavender-herbs/

Free Homemade Gift Ideas. Instructions for Easy Homemade Gifts to Make. (n.d.). Homemade-Gifts-Made-Easy.com. Retrieved from https://www.homemade-gifts-made-easy.com/

Harvesting Fresh Lavender: How to Harvest, Prune & Dry Lavender Flowers. (2020, July 8). Homestead and Chill. https://homesteadandchill.com/how-to-harvest-dry-lavender/

History & Uses of Lavender - Lavender | Lavender Sense browse. (n.d.). Www.lavendersense.com. Retrieved from http://www.lavendersense.com/index.php/Lavender/Index

How To Choose The Best Lavender. (2014). Americanmeadows.com. https://www.americanmeadows.com/perennials/lavender/how-to-choose-the-best-lavender

How to choose the right Lavender? (n.d.). Gardenia.net. https://www.gardenia.net/guide/how-to-choose-the-right-lavender

How to Grow Lavender | Lavender Planting & Growing Tips. (n.d.). Bonnie Plants. Retrieved from https://bonnieplants.com/how-to-grow/growing-lavender

How to Grow Lavender in Every Climate | Gardener's Path. (2019, February 2). Gardener's Path. https://gardenerspath.com/plants/herbs/grow-lavender/

How to Make Homemade Lavender Oil & 9 Ways to Use It. (2020, July 25). Homestead and Chill. https://homesteadandchill.com/homemade-lavender-oil/

https://www.facebook.com/thespruceofficial. (2019). *Pruning Lavender Promotes Good Flowering and Long Life.* The Spruce. https://www.thespruce.com/how-to-prune-lavender-3269538

Laura. (2016, November 10). *12 Easy Lavender Crafts and DIY.* Baking Outside the Box. https://www.bakingoutsidethebox.com/12-easy-lavender-crafts-diy/

Lavender lime potpourri recipe | Dried Flower Craft. (2012, March 1). https://driedflowercraft.co.uk/2012/03/lavender-lime-potpourri-recipe/

Lavender Oil for Skin: Uses and Benefits. (2018, December 17). Healthline. https://www.healthline.com/health/lavender-oil-for-skin#summary

Literally Everything You Need To Know About The Oils Vs. Essential Oils Debate. (n.d.). The Zoe Report. Retrieved from https://www.thezoereport.com/p/oils-vs-essential-oils-the-biggest-differences-the-most-popular-uses-more-19442788

Perry, D. (n.d.). *How to Cook With Lavender so Your Food Doesn't Taste Like Soap.* Bon Appétit. Retrieved from https://www.bonappetit.com/test-kitchen/how-to/article/cooking-with-lavender

Piccolo, M. (2018, October 11). *5 Easy Methods of Drying Lavender at Home.* DryingAllFoods. https://www.dryingallfoods.com/drying-lavender/

Planting and Caring for Lavender in Pots. (n.d.). Gardenia.net. Retrieved from https://www.gardenia.net/guide/planting-and-caring-for-lavender-in-pots

Problems With Lavender Plants. (n.d.). Garden Guides. Retrieved from https://www.gardenguides.com/83628-problems-lavender-plants.html

Pruning Your Lavender Plants. (n.d.). Gardenia.net. Retrieved from https://www.gardenia.net/guide/pruning-your-lavender-plants

Stradley, L. (2015, April 22). *Culinary Lavender.* What's Cooking America. https://whatscookingamerica.net/Lavender.htm

The History of Lavender. (2019). Tumalolavender.com. https://www.tumalolavender.com/article-history-of-lavender.htm

www.ingramcontent.com/pod-product-compliance
Lightning Source LLC
LaVergne TN
LVHW051916060526
838200LV00004B/167